FLYING COMBAT AIRCRAFT OF THE USAAF-USAF

THE IOWA STATE UNIVERSITY PRESS / AMES, IOWA

1 9 7 5

FLYING COMBAT AIRCRAFT OF THE USAAF-USAF

edited by

Robin Higham / Abigail T. Siddall

AEROSPACE HISTORIAN, sponsor of this book, is an international journal for aerospace history and the official journal of the Air Force Historical Foundation. Established in 1954, it has been published since June 1970 at the Department of History, Kansas State University, Manhattan, Kansas 66506.

This book, the first of a proposed series on American aircraft, is designed to help readers of all ages appreciate the role USAAF-USAF combat aircraft have played in our country's history and respect the gallant men who have flown them in times of war and peace.

By obtaining such personal recollections now, our knowledge of these memorable times can be preserved for the future.

Composed and printed by
The Iowa State University Press
Ames, Iowa 50010.

First edition, 1975

Library of Congress Cataloging in Publication Data
Main entry under title:

Flying combat aircraft of the USAAF-USAF.

1. Airplanes, Military—History. 2. Aeronautics, Military—United States—History. I. Higham, Robin D. S. II. Siddall, Abigail T., 1930–
UG1243.F55 358.41'8'3 75-8932
ISBN 0-8138-0325-X

CONTENTS

PREFACE

THE informative and entertaining pieces presented here are both original documents and fallible memoirs. It is admitted at once that they represent one school of thought only as to the proper way to handle a particular plane. Another pilot in another war theater may have flown the craft quite differently (or thought he did), so no claim is made that these chapters are absolutely reliable guides. We do say each has been prepared both conscientiously and lovingly and has, whenever possible, been checked against an appropriate authoritative manual.

We acknowledge also that an ingredient of flying life is the tendency to "shoot a line." Thus, even though the authors believe some of the stories related here to be completely accurate, they may not be. In any event, we hope readers will find these accounts enlightening, stimulating, and sometimes amusing—all to be recalled, in the case of veterans at least, with fond memories, if not complete agreement.

To include chapters on all combat aircraft was of course impossible because of lack of space and the difficulty of finding authors. We hope to correct omissions in a subsequent volume.

Unless otherwise indicated, all photographs are courtesy of the United States Air Force.

R. H. AND A. T. S.

FLAP WARNING
FLAPS MUST BE EXTENDED
RADIO CALL
467780
PROPELLER R.P.M. LIMIT

Mitchell bomber flies over North African desert in 1942 en route to the target for the day. Note shadows cast by preceding formation.

B-25 Mitchell

ARTHUR J. THOMAS

MUCH has been written about the combat record of the B-25 Mitchell medium bomber, and its successes in World War II are well documented. Those who flew a B-25 in battle can still today make a keen showing in competition with "Jug" jockies, Lightning riders, and P-51 pushers when it comes to retelling hair-raising tales. The initial U.S. Army contract for 148 Mitchells was awarded to North American in September 1939, and the first B-25 was test flown in September 1940. (Compare that with today's lead time on new aircraft!) Subsequently many models evolved with changes and improvements dictated by combat experience. Among the long list of firsts accredited to the B-25 are: first to see action on all fronts; first to pack a 75-mm cannon; first Army airplane to sink an enemy sub; first medium bomber to fly from a carrier deck; and first U.S. plane over Tokyo.

But let us look at her twilight years (1945 through the late 1950s) when the "Baker Two Bits," as she was affectionally known, served as the backbone of the Air Force's multiengine pilot training program.

In the pilot training program established in 1939 there was no provision for separate training of pilots for two-engine aircraft. Soon after World War II began in Europe, however, such a program was initiated; by Pearl Harbor, aviation cadets were receiving advanced training in B-18s at Barksdale Field, Louisiana. Seven multiengine bases operated eventually. To augment the supply of trainers, commercial types were accepted by the Air Corps—mainly the Beech AT-10 and the Cessna AT-17. Because the Curtiss AT-9 was an all-metal craft (thus difficult to procure), its use was limited, even though it was the best two-engine trainer at the time.

In late 1942 exhaustive tests were made using the B-25; they proved that students with limited knowledge and average skill could readily learn to handle the plane. General use of the B-25 for training started in July 1943, and by May 1945 all multiengine training was accomplished in this airplane. Redesignated as the TB-25 and downgraded from "medium" to "light" bomber in descriptive phraseology, the trainer provided an excellent student learning tool.

By 1950 the TB-25 had to be considered an old aircraft, particularly when compared with the current combat types of the day. A popular comment at the time (paraphrasing a more dramatic speech) stated in effect, "Old airplanes never die, they just get turned over to the Training Command." True, heaters didn't always work; many windows were checked and crazed, limiting visibility; starters burned up; cylinders cracked; spark plugs glassed over and became glow plugs in the Texas dust; and instructors on the whole seemed to be determined to log as much single-engine time as multiengine time. However, techniques of multiengine flying acquired in this program were carried over and applied to the newer, heavier, and hotter aircraft flown even today in the USAF.

B-25 students and instructors of the 1950s remember the bases in Texas and Oklahoma with acres and acres of concrete ramp and anywhere from 85 to 135 airplanes staked out. Most were J models, with a few Ks and some L, M, and N model series. The latter models had such goodies as more nosewheel tread on the runway, larger escape hatches, Holley carburetors, relocated feathering buttons, cockpit lighting, and more advanced electrical panels and navigation equipment.

Each plane approximated 33,000 pounds for takeoff, was 53 feet 6 inches long with a span of 67 feet 7 inches, and stood 16 feet 4 inches high. It was a big machine for students previously familiar with such types as the Stearman PT-18, Taylorcraft TG-6, and perhaps the North American T-28A. It was powered by two Wright Cyclone engines rated at 1,700 hp each on 100/130 octane fuel, having two-speed centrifugal impeller blowers with ratios of approximately 7:1 and 10:1. With a 974-gallon fuel capacity, endurance approximated six and one-half hours—longer of course with long-range economy power settings.

Oddly enough, this was one airplane in which range could be slightly extended by lowering one-quarter flaps. At an economical cruise setting (160 mph) the aircraft maintained altitude in a slightly nose-high attitude. Because the fuel tank outlet was located in the forward portion of the tank, this nose-high condition made about 40 gallons of fuel unavailable. Lowering the flaps raised the tail of the aircraft, and the fuel could then be used, easing the fuel shortage tensions that sometimes permeated the cockpit toward the end of a westbound, headwind-plagued flight.

We soon learned not to rely too heavily on this extra reserve fuel. An instructor with two students on a weekend cross-country to Florida departed Reese Air Force Base one Friday night and made it to West Palm Beach Air Force Base nonstop with an adequate fuel reserve. Reluctant to leave the glorious beaches and the even more glorious girls thereon, they delayed the departure from West Palm until late Sunday afternoon. To cover up they decided to make a nonstop flight home. About 40 minutes east of Lubbock Texas, the flaps were lowered; 20 minutes later No. 2 engine died of starvation; 10 minutes later they were safely on the ground at Lubbock Municipal Airport—10 miles short of destination. A quick purchase of 50 gallons of gas for cash and a safe landing at Reese shortly thereafter would make a nice ending to a hairy story. But who just happened to be at the Municipal Airport that night? None other than Colonel C. P. West, base commander at Reese. His inquisitiveness about the fact that one of his B-25s landed at another airport with one engine feathered and that cash was being paid out of the crew's pockets for 50 gallons of fuel must be commended. The next morning we had a new maintenance officer at Reese—the flight instructor involved became the flight line fuel servicing officer.

B-25 Mitchell bomber with antiflak bombs bursting prematurely in midair. The bombs would have covered the German antiaircraft batteries with dense smoke to permit better bombing of the Ora rail yards on the Brenner route in 1944.

In approaching the TB-25 for the first time, one could not resist the feeling of awe it inspired! It was more than a great big T-6 with two of everything. It had bomb bay doors, gun turret positions, a bombardier's position in a glass nose, engine nacelles that looked as big as the T-6 fuselage and emitted a mighty roar as the upperclassmen applied power for takeoff from the nearby runway. Perhaps even a little apprehension was mixed with the awe when we realized that during the next 110 hours of flying time we would have to become intimately familiar with this machine. At this point mastery of emergency procedures, formation flying, navigation, and instrument flying seemed a formidable task indeed.

Our instructor, Captain Billie D. Smith, was certainly one of the "old pros" at instructing. Like many of the Reese instructor pilots at the time, he was a recent returnee from the Korean conflict, a very capable B-25 pilot, and most adept at analyzing student errors and unspoken thoughts.

The initial "dollar" ride was truly a joy! Apparently sensing our misgivings, Captain Billie D. capitalized on them. His personal competence

D day in the South Pacific, with a momentary junction of American air and sea forces on the move. B-25s are en route to Rabaul to blast Japanese airfields; the invasion convoy several thousand feet below is spreading toward Green Island.

and confidence in the airplane were reassuring and his enthusiasm most contagious. One of his first "pearls of wisdom" was the fact that "North American engineers put propellers on the B-25 just to keep the pilots cool." To prove his point he feathered No. 1, and sure enough the neophyte pilot in the left seat at the time began to sweat profusely. Nonsense, of course, but just what was needed to establish the desired rapport. (I have since used this gimmick with new students of my own many times and have found it always works; "student sweat" is a most effective ice breaker. No pun intended.) This sense of humor cropped up repeatedly during the next six months with Billie D., particularly when the situation was looking most grim from a student standpoint.

While that engine was feathered, each of us had the opportunity to crawl into the seat and make steep turns (60° bank) both left and right. This just had to be verboten—we had known for years that no pilot ever made steep turns with an engine out, and certainly turning into the dead engine was just plain asking for it. Imagine our surprise and chagrin when we found that it could be done, and all hands survived! Billie D. explained that the maneuver could be accomplished safely if done properly. This led into my being talked through a single-engine stall, and although we wallowed around the sky a good bit, the point was made that "the safe single-engine speed on the B-25 is 145 mph." We were told in dead seriousness never to forget that fact, and I never have. At 140 mph, directional control was tricky, to say the least. Between 130 and 135 it was well-nigh impossible. Below that, you just went where the airplane wanted to go until the airspeed was increased and/or power on the good engine was reduced.

Billie D. promised us that if ever he read less than 145 mph on the airspeed indicator (except on the short final of a landing approach or during an intentional stall series) he would guarantee us the loss of power on one engine or the other. He kept that promise several times.

I didn't get caught with a slow airspeed until several months later, during the instrument flying phase of training. When our group had about six or seven hours of basic instrument training, our instructor found the situation he had been looking for: visibility through the Texas Panhandle was reduced to 3 miles in dust and at Armarillo further reduced by moderate snow showers. While we didn't think we were quite ready for low-frequency range approaches, Captain Billie D. just couldn't pass up such a good opportunity.

En route to Amarillo I kept hoping we'd get there between showers and it wouldn't be too bad. As if reading my mind, Billie D., with a big grin on his face, hollered across the cockpit, "Buck up, things are going to get worse!" And they did. At Amarillo we encountered thunder and lightning, snow and dust, static on the radio, light turbulence (it seemed more like severe turbulence), brown slush on the windshield, and possibly more brown slush on the student pilot's seat.

While I was trying to decide whether to follow the close-in range pro-

Rabaul Harbor, showing Japanese ships hit by 1,000-pound bombs dropped by B-25s.

cedure or turn outbound for a procedure turn, a quick glance at the airspeed indicator (showing 142 mph) explained the sudden loss of power from the left engine. If ever a naive, overburdened student compounded his problems by his own ineptness, this was the time. The only help from the right seat came in the form of an admonition to "maintain control of the aircraft." By the time the "dead leg, dead throttle, simulate feather" emergency checklist was completed, I was completely lost. Flying was like wallowing around inside a great big bottle of chocolate milk—I couldn't see anything, I was not too sure which way was up, and I certainly had no idea where the range station might be.

Ground controllers at Amarillo in those days were apparently used to Reese students floundering around in their airspace and indicated no concern. A glance at our jolly instructor prompted the thought, "That idiot over there is actually enjoying this." Thirty minutes or so later, when the field finally came into sight, I too began to enjoy the flight. Captain Smith was so right when he said, "You'll never know if you can make an actual instrument approach until you make one."

This also was a turning point in the student-machine relationship. No longer was the TB-25 a formidable adversary that had to be conquered. Now it was to become a partner in developing skills and techniques that would lead to higher, faster flights over great distances.

The TB-25 was noisy, very noisy. Most instructor pilots suffered some permanent hearing loss during a two- to three-year tour of duty. Furthermore, temperature in the cockpit was uncomfortable—too cold in winter and very hot during Texas summers. On the plus side of the ledger, the cockpit was roomy enough for comfortable seating with adequate cushions. (Big instructors carried a personal seat cushion, little instructors carried two or more.) Head room and leg room were more than ample, and visibility was excellent. And the airplane was "honest" to the extent that an experienced instructor could predict to a very fine degree just how far he could let a student go before corrective action was required to preclude an uncontrollable situation.

Cockpit of B-25 showing control knobs and instrument panels with dual interchangeable flight instruments for pilot and copilot.

Although the supply of parts dried up during the last couple of years the TB-25 was in service, maintenance was remarkably good. Utilization approximated eight hours per day, five days a week. Engines withstood the student abuse of rapid power changes, much time at the higher power settings due to frequent takeoffs and landings, and single-engine practice. Airframes were subjected to "bone rattling" hard landings and the severe buffeting of power-on full breaking stalls followed by secondary stalls when too abrupt a recovery was attempted. Occasionally single-engine stalls resulted in an inverted stall attitude when the student failed to reduce power on the good engine quickly enough. Weather avoidance radar was not yet available, so it was not unusual to plow through a Gulf Coast thunderstorm on a night cross-country. With all this, actual engine failures were rare; with the exception of occasional superficial hail damage or an antenna fused by lightning, structural failures were practically nonexistent.

The TB-25 was safe, simple, and forgiving. At the same time it was complex enough to require learning the effects of a power loss; aircraft configuration versus performance; emergency or alternate operation of landing gear, flaps, hydraulic system, and air brakes; and fuel management

with a cross-feed system. These things, learned well, have made a significant contribution to USAF's operational success in more modern multiengine aircraft.

LT. COL. ARTHUR J. THOMAS, a glider pilot in World War II, served as an all-weather radar-intercept observer and directed a test program for an electronic aerial geodetic survey system before retiring from the USAF in 1971. He is currently a student in landscape architecture at Kansas State University and maintains an active status in civilian flying.

High above an Allied convoy in 1944, a group of B-26s head for Europe to bomb Hitler's crumbling defense system.

B-26 Marauder

DOUGLAS C. CONLEY

THE B-26 was a World War II medium bomber with twin Pratt & Whitney radial engines (R-2800) equipped with four-blade Curtiss electric propellers. It was designed for low-altitude bombing, but a high loss rate in low-altitude combat forced us to operate it at 12,000 feet. The craft carried a crew of seven and a normal load of four 1,000-pound bombs. It had a cigar-shaped fuselage and short stubby wings, and it was fast and "hot" for its time. At this time, in the more or less embryonic world of flight, an aircraft that landed at a high rate of speed was referred to as "hot." The principal difference between the B-26 and most other aircraft of its day was a landing speed about 20 mph faster and a cruise speed comparable to the fastest fighter aircraft. This increased speed coupled with a higher wing loading represented an advancement from the design standpoint and confronted pilots with a whole new ball game in the art of flying. The first B-26s stalled at 130 mph, came "unstuck" from the ground at 135, and cruised at 220 mph indicated; instantaneous engine failure precipitated a vicious control problem.

The stubby wings were responsible for her nickname of "Flying Prostitute"—she had no (or very little) visible means of support. The serious control problem upon engine failure earned her the name "the Martin Murderer," and the reputation of "a Marauder a day in Tampa Bay" was assigned to her at about the time I began flying her in the fall of 1942.

In spite of this I loved her, as did nearly every pilot who flew her. In all honesty, however, there were a few pilots who had great difficulty checking out in a B-26 at McDill, probably because of her reputation. A performance average of one crash a day from unknown causes and with all hands killed is reason enough to make anyone jumpy, and I must admit to considerable apprehension on each takeoff.

I reported to McDill Field at Tampa in September 1942, proud of my new silver wings and my recent promotion to SSgt Pilot. (We received many faltering uncertain salutes from old line chiefs because of the pilot's wings in spite of the SSgt insignia.) Upon graduation from flying school we had received our assignments, and although disappointed at not getting fighters we were resigned to flying the B-17 (reportedly at McDill). Imagine our chagrin to discover upon arrival that there were no B-17s in sight but B-26s everywhere. We were already aware of the B-26's reputation for being dangerous, a reputation undoubtedly embellished for shock effect during "hangar flying" bull sessions throughout the Air Corps. With the hope that the rumors might not be true, I began dual flight instruction to check out as first pilot.

Each transition flight carried an instructor and two student pilots, who took turns taking off and landing. Because of control problems accompanying engine failure, we were required to fly a rather peculiar flight pattern. On takeoff we made a long low run to assure earliest gaining of flight speed sufficient to provide maximum airflow over the control surfaces, so that the sharp control movement required to counter the effects of engine failure would not be so likely to result in a high-speed stall. Most aircraft flew a few miles out over the swamp before attempting to gain more than 50 feet of altitude. After the climb to pattern altitude we reduced to the final approach airspeed of 140 mph indicated and made what was called a one-shot approach and landing: at 140 mph without using power to drag it in or to delay the stall after round-out, a pilot had only one chance to put the aircraft in proper position for landing before the stall occurred. When the far end of the runway disappeared below the nose, we cut all power, nosed over, and made our round-out and touchdown without the aid of

B-26 Marauder in flight.

power. Fortunately, old Glen L's people designed her with one of the sturdiest landing gears I have ever seen. There were no touch-and-gos; we taxied back to the takeoff area after every landing, and the crew chief got out to perform a walk-around inspection before the next takeoff.

After we had shot a few landings, the instructor pilot got out. The other student and I then took the aircraft up for a few stalls and practice landings, alternating in the pilot's seat. The other student pilot made me extremely nervous by the careless way he flew the aircraft—riding the burble of a stall, as it were, almost continuously in the pattern. I expressed my concern to him in no uncertain terms. We didn't crash.

The next day I was assigned a different student pilot to continue our familiarization program. We went out over Tampa Bay to practice stalls and single-engine procedures, and we found that the B-26 actually flew well on one engine, provided care was used in shutting the engine down and feathering the propeller. After completing this air work we headed back to McDill to shoot some landings. Upon approaching the field we observed a large plume of black smoke rising from the middle of the field and suspected the worst. I discovered upon landing that the student pilot I had checked out with the day before had "spun in" to crash, and all on board had perished.

While I was at McDill, one of our older pilots, a captain in his mid-twenties, achieved the then unheard-of distinction of surviving a crash in a B-26: he had a runaway propeller and belly-landed in a swamp. The R-2800 engine was very reliable and seldom failed, but the electric propeller was another matter. It was responsible for most of the crashes. Carbon brushes on a slip ring transmitted the electric power to change the pitch on the prop. This mechanism was new and unfamiliar, and it was the maintenance man's nightmare. Dirty brushes and changing clearance due to wear resulted in the loss of many aircraft. The high-pitched screech caused by a runaway propeller could be heard for miles. A break in electrical contact caused the propeller to go immediately to flat pitch, and an extreme overspeed condition resulted. When this happened there was suddenly no thrust from that engine—with the same effect as engine failure.

The design of the aircraft was responsible for the control problem resulting from engine failure. The cylindrical fuselage required engine placement well out on the wing to provide clearance for the large propellers. (A flat-sided fuselage like that on the B-25 would have provided the same functional space internally but would not have extended so far out toward the wing.) With the two engines so far from the centerline of the fuselage and so far from each other, we had to contend with extreme aerodynamic forces when one quit suddenly while the other was still churning. The wing on the failed side immediately "fell back" and stalled while the good engine torque and thrust worked the opposite effect with the other wing. The result was a snap roll. Admittedly, the above is "lay" reasoning, but to me it explains the probable cause of the tendency to flip when an engine failed.

We moved from McDill to Lakeland, Florida, for combat crew training. As pilots and maintenance personnel became more proficient, the accident rate declined dramatically. After forming our crews, we practiced skip bombing and .50-caliber target practice on dye markers dropped in the gulf. I was fortunate to be assigned the best crew in the Air Force.

While at Lakeland I had an experience with weight and balance of the B-26. One day when we were walking out to the aircraft for a practice bombing mission, an airman asked if he could go along for the ride. I told him he could hop up in back with the gunner. We almost finished that takeoff in the company of angels. There were twelve 100-pound practice bombs in the front bomb bay and ten in the back; with the addition of one extra man in the back, the plane was very tail heavy. The first inkling of this condition came at about 90 mph when I lifted the nosewheel off. To my surprise, the nosewheel kept coming up and at such a rate that I had to shove forward quickly to keep the tail from dragging the runway. In retrospect I should have chopped power immediately, taxied back, and reconfigured my load; instinctively, more or less, I decided to try to fly her in that condition, so I let her roll and build up speed. (Looking back today from a position of maturity and experience, I am horrified at that decision.) At the time, the engines were developing full power; my sense of control was improving with each second as the speed increased, and I felt I could fly her off and reconfigure my load in the air. On the theory that any decision resulting in success is a good decision, I made a good decision. She overcame the stalled angle of attack at 160 mph, just before we ran out of runway, and struggled into the air riding on the burble of a stall just above the pine trees. My knuckles were white on the control wheel, and I'm glad I didn't have a mirror to see the look of terror on my face; I made my sigh of relief as inaudible as possible so as not to alarm Junior (my copilot) unduly. When I moved my passenger from the rear to the front, the plane flew beautifully.

We moved from Lakeland to Lake Charles, Louisiana, to fly tactical missions in support of the mock war being staged by the "Red" and "Blue" forces of the U.S. Army. Having done one stint at maneuvers in the Louisiana swamps while a squad leader in the combat engineers, I thoroughly relished dive-bombing the "ground pounders" with small paper bags filled with flour. As we approached a marching column walking down a dirt road, we could see them dive for the ditches and cover as we flew over skimming the treetops. Our group commander, in keeping with the low-altitude design of the B-26, told us when we began the maneuvers that he didn't want to see a damn one of us above 500 feet unless we were in the traffic pattern. Since buzzing was and is illegal, this was all we needed to turn a chore into an exhilarating adventure. We cut grass in level pastures, made wakes on water with prop wash, and straddled lone pine trees with our props. Junior tried to get me to fly under the Port Arthur bridge; all the crew agreed except Starky, our navigator, so we never did it.

At Lake Charles I learned by mistake a peculiarity of the B-26 that was later to save my life. Too steep an approach and too sudden a roundout (at the right altitude, luckily) and she shuddered from a high-speed stall, sat down, and stuck. I later used this feature when belly-landing, after combat damage, in a vineyard that was too small to land in.

We checked out our copilots at Lake Charles. I drilled Junior repeatedly by telling him every move to make, and if he didn't do it at the right time I did it for him. He rounded out high and stayed there until I let it down; he bounced it in, overshot, undershot, etc., until it looked hopeless. I finally realized my method of instruction was becoming counterproductive because he was waiting to be told to make every move. On the next landing I told him he was flying with an armless deaf-mute and he had to make a good landing or kill us all. He made a good one and had it "made" from that time on.

From Lake Charles we went to Savannah to pick up new B-26s to ferry overseas to combat. We hopped down to West Palm Beach for our leaping-off point, and while there we named our aircraft *Phoebe* and painted the name under the window by each crew station. She was a good bird; she got 65 missions in before being demolished in a belly-landing after combat damage.

Upon arrival at Oran in northeast Africa our beloved *Phoebe* was assigned to another crew; our crew was split up, and the veteran combat copilots were given crews of their own. (It was a personal tragedy to lose a crew who had flown together through training and whose teamwork and demonstrated proficiency had convinced us they were the best crew, to a man, in the whole damned Air Corps.) The veteran combat copilots had an average of eight missions. They had crowded in a lot of experience in those eight missions. They had tried low altitude with six-ship formations; after losing all aircraft to deadly antiaircraft fire they were flying at 12,000 feet by the time I got there. The ex-copilot, J.C., who was now my first pilot, was a pretty darned good pilot. He had about 10 hours of first-pilot time and I had over 300.

We were returning from our second combat mission when I noticed the oil pressure falling off on the right engine. The oil temperature did not rise, nor did the cylinder head temperature, so I concluded that the oil pressure gauge was faulty. But we were losing oil, as we were to discover shortly. We were letting down in a six-ship formation to enter the pattern to land; we were the left wingman, lead element, in a left turn at a comfortable 200 mph when the right engine froze with a sudden, final shudder. As quickly as we perceived what had happened, both the pilot and I stomped the left rudder to the floor; the plane did a half snap roll right through the middle of the formation, past the nose of the No. 4 aircraft, and ended up in a vertical right turn. I never saw our formation, during or after our recovery, because I was completely occupied with trying to regain control. (I can only imagine what would happen shortly after take-off at low airspeed if an engine froze.) Now for one of those rare single-engine landings to get her down safely. J.C.'s face had an ashen pallor, and again I was glad there was no mirror to reflect my own color. Something about the look on his face and the way his knees were shaking struck me as funny, and I managed something less than a hearty laugh. I'm sure this helped to relieve the tension as we set about trimming her up and preparing to land.

I had long before worked out a single-engine procedure to use if necessary: no go-around, no dragging her in at low speed on one fan. We picked the nearest runway, approached high and fast, and set her down across traffic. The rest of the returning aircraft were landing on the runway perpendicular to ours at 30-second intervals. We could not raise the tower to interrupt the flow of cross-traffic, and when a collision looked inevitable at the intersection, J.C. opened the throttle on the good engine to full power. This accelerated us enough to pass in front of the approaching aircraft, but it also caused us to jump up on one wing from the sudden torque. We made it.

While flying with this same pilot I had another experience with

A direct hit from enemy flak penetrated the left engine of this B-26 during a U.S. attack against German front-line communications center in the path of advancing First and Ninth armies.

weight and balance. We were approaching Pantelleria for a bombing run with a bomb load of four 1,000-pounders and an extra crewman, a photographer. As we crossed the IP inbound, the photographer quietly went to the rear compartment to record the bomb strikes from the camera hatch. Suddenly the airspeed fell toward a stall. Since there was no ready explanation for it, there was panic in the cockpit—at least for a moment. J.C. added full power to no avail, and the formation was passing us by as if we were standing still. I never felt a stall approaching, but because we were not gaining speed at full power J.C. salvoed the bombs, dived out of the area, and headed home. Then it occurred to us we had too much weight in the tail. We brought the cameraman up front, and that (or the now empty bomb bays) corrected the weight and balance problem. We chalked that one up to the cost of learning.

Later J.C. and I were given a crew to share. He would fly pilot on one mission and I would fly the next one. One day J.C. was flying: the flak was intense, and we had numerous holes in our aircraft; our airspeed and hydraulic systems had been shot out; to cap it off, as we returned to base across the Mediterranean, bad weather caused us to lose sight of our formation. As wingmen, without a navigator, we were lost. As our fuel got low, we sighted the North African Coast, but it was completely unfamiliar. We decided to belly her in before we ran out of fuel, while we could still choose the pasture where we wanted to land. I suggested to J.C. that we "drag" a farmer's field that looked level—near a town so we could get help if we were bleeding.

We decided to go in with wheels up (a brilliant decision, since we had no hydraulics to lower the gear), and I would cut off all electrical power on final. Also, just before touchdown I was to feather the props to keep a blade from shearing and coming through the fuselage.

J.C. buzzed the field from about 500 feet to his satisfaction; since I was expecting him to go across at about 10 feet, I was surprised to hear him say, "I'm on final, cut the power!" I turned off the master switches, waited a moment, and hit the feathering buttons; the props didn't feather of course because they were electrically operated, but by this time I was too preoccupied with the approaching touchdown to correct the error. Perhaps terrified would be a better word: the "field" was a vineyard with short tree-sized stumps of old grapevines, and we were coming in cross-furrow. Worse yet, when we leveled at about 3 feet to play out our speed, the field suddenly seemed to shrink in length until collision with the sharply raised roadbed at the end appeared inevitable. Almost instinctively I yelled at J.C. to snap-stall her in. He apparently had not experienced what the B-26 would do under those circumstances, so he just sat there continuing to play her speed out, as it were. I waited a microsecond or two for him to move, but when he didn't I grabbed the control column and snapped it back in my lap. She shuddered and sat down immediately. She skidded on her belly for perhaps a hundred yards, slewed around to point in the opposite direction, sheared off a prop blade which went through the fuselage behind my head, and stopped just short of the embankment. The engines were almost torn from their mounts, but the fuselage was intact. No one was hurt—a remarkable fact which attests to the B-26's structural integrity. People came to help almost immediately; so we posted a civilian policeman to guard the wreckage, borrowed a truck, and drove to our base (which turned out to be just over a small range of mountains). The miracle of adrenalin was demonstrated to me that evening. I was on an unbelievable "high"—keenly alert and filled with boundless energy—until all of a sudden, in fact in moments, my energy drained from me with such a rush I could hardly make it to my bunk before collapsing from exhaustion.

There are many stories of how well the B-26 did in combat—coming back with unbelievable damage, making two-wheel landings and subsequent cartwheels with no one killed, and so on. She was a sturdy craft that demanded skill in emergencies, but she was sweet to handle—the real seat-of-the-pants feel to flying was there. She did beautiful wingovers. My favorite "exuberance" maneuvers were a dive followed by a vertical climb and a negative G pushover describing a perfect half-circle to level flight at a speed across the top a fraction ahead of a stall; or a dive followed by a vertical climb to near stall as she did a slow wingover through the top of a brilliantly white cumulus cloud. As a pilot gained experience in the B-26, he could "strap her on his back," become integrated with her, fly formation within inches of the lead aircraft and never vary the distance, and "grease" her in on landing with a featherlike touchdown time after time.

Years later I visited the Air Force Museum to see the B-26 on display there. As I walked around her, memories came back of the people I flew with and the many successful flights she carried us through. My vision blurred as I gave free rein to thoughts of another day in time and space and I took a flight on the wings of nostalgia.

In World War II LT. COL. DOUGLAS C. CONLEY flew a B-26 from North Africa and Sardinia in operations over Italy and southern France. He received a battlefield commission as Second Lieutenant in 1943 and retired in 1973 after more than 32 years of active service in the USAF.

B-29 Superfortress in flight. First flown in 1942, it saw action both in World War II and in Korea.

B-29 Superfortress

HAYWOOD S. HANSELL, JR.

FOR the pilots and crews who flew the Superfortress in 1945 there was a word that described her simply and well—the same word that would have come immediately to the mind of an old line cavalryman: she was a thoroughbred. Like her smaller sister the B-17, she could take an astonishing amount of punishment and still keep flying till she brought you home. No mean quirks. No faltering at the hurdles. Whatever the obstacle ahead, you knew without question she would have a go at it. She was big and lithe and beautiful and very powerful. And like the old line cavalryman, the pilot came to be a part of his mount. Maybe it was a matter of smooth vibration from her four powerful engines when you had them synchronized. I don't know whether other pilots of multiengine aircraft got the same message that engine drone carried to me, but I had only to think of a song to have it picked up and sung to me by the rhythm of the engines. It was pleasant but likely to be dangerous, because it became a lullaby that put me comfortably to sleep.

General Arnold had taken the most daring and farsighted logistics decision of the war. Before the B-29 had even had her first flight he had authorized enormous factories for mass production. She was all new: four new engines of unprecedented power (Wright R-3350 with 2,200 hp each), a pressurized cabin, remotely controlled guns, cruising altitude and speed and range far higher than her predecessors. And to cap it all she was to operate unescorted, in spite of the European experience with bombers versus fighters, against the Japanese homelands. She faced a tight strategic schedule to operate from bases not yet captured but 1,500 miles away from her targets.

She was initially conceived as an all-weather bomber, operating preferably at night and in cloud cover, using a new radar bombsight. She did operate in this mode from bases in China and later from the Marianas. But the task initially assigned her from the Marianas called for destruction of small targets not easily identified by radar, so it became necessary to rely on visual precision bombing in daylight, at least in the initial phase.

This of course had all kinds of effects upon her as a bomber. The first was a radical change in her armament. The first B-29s had twin .50-caliber guns in the top forward turret. But experience with daylight bombing in Europe indicated that the most vulnerable quarter of attack from fighters was from the front. I cringe to confess that I chaired a committee that insisted on changing the forward top turret from two to four .50-caliber guns. The change ruined a beautiful cockpit by installing a large ammunition drum which took up all the room and blocked movement in all directions. The navigator-radar operator could barely squeeze by to reach his station. The weight went up considerably too, although the four-gun turret was near enough to the center of lift not to cause serious problems in longitudinal balance.

I shall never forget my introduction to the B-29. I was Chief of Staff of the Twentieth Air Force when General Arnold, its Commander in Chief, sent me to a modification center at Birmingham, Alabama, to try to straighten out a production jam. There were many B-29s on the field waiting for installation of armament not yet available. Meanwhile the Training Command was screaming for B-29s for crew training. I arranged to release some B-29s, with incomplete armament, to the Training Command and was about to return to Washington when it occurred to me that this was a good chance to get in a little B-29 flight time. I mentioned this, and presently a young captain taxied one up to the operations office. He tried his best to get me to sit in the airplane commander's seat, on the left, but I firmly declined. I suggested that we go over to an auxiliary field and perhaps I'd swap seats with him there.

The pilot's compartment was a new and strange environment for me. In the B-17 you sat in a comfortable seat and looked forward through a nearly vertical windshield just up front of you and along the nose of the fuselage. You had a reference point to adjust to the horizon. But in the B-29 you sat down in the curved nose of the airplane and there was no nearly vertical curved shield—only a series of small panes stretching out in front of you. Furthermore, there was no nose of the fuselage along which you could look as a reference. After a while you adjusted to this, but initially it was confusing and uncomfortable, and there was a tendency to fly on instruments even in clear weather.

We went over to the auxiliary field and made a few landings and swapped seats. I tried a couple of landings, with indifferent success, and suggested that we go back to Birmingham, where I had a stripped-down B-17 staff plane. He suggested that I fly back to Birmingham, but I objected. Birmingham has pretty good sized hills around it, and I didn't relish finding a cloud with rocks in it. Besides I wasn't at all sure I could get the airplane down successfully. But he kept insisting that I could do it, and I was ashamed to admit that I couldn't, so I gave it a try. I got down all right, with no greater damage than chagrin over the trail of blue smoke hovering over the runway, produced by burning rubber when I used all the brakes she had to keep from running beyond the end of the strip. After taxiing back I rose to get out while the captain was filling out the Form-1. He turned to me and asked, "General, how much time have you got in B-29s?" I said, "I don't know. Whatever it is, you just got it." He turned pale and said in a shaken voice, "My God, General! I'm not fully checked out on this airplane."

One effect of this experience was to convince me not to take any more

Flight engineer's compartment aboard a B-29.

foolish chances. I got permission to take a "crash" checkout course at Roswell, New Mexico. In five days, during which I put in what seemed like 150 hours of work both in ground school and in flying, I learned a lot of things I hadn't known. In the first place I learned that the B-29 was a military command—not just an airplane. It was something like a naval ship, in which many people had to work as a team. Maybe Jimmy Doolittle could have flown it alone, but not us lesser mortals. The pilot, the copilot, and the flight engineers all had specific, coordinated functions in flying the airplane. The airplane commander called for power settings and wing flap settings and cowl flap settings and landing gear settings, much as the captain of a ship calls for engine performance and wheel corrections. The gunners had flight functions as lookouts, since the pilots could not see toward the rear quarters. And of course they had responsibilities for their remotely controlled guns, which had to be properly stowed for takeoff. The idea of ship command was deliberately fostered. The crew lined up at the left front position of the airplane for formal inspection by the airplane commander prior to entering the aircraft. Inspection checks and responses by intercoms were precisely prescribed and precisely performed.

The checklist dialogue between pilot and copilot was extensive: 16 questions, checks, and answers before entering the airplane; 25 before starting the engines; 9 before taxiing; 12 before takeoff; 13 before landing. The flight engineer responded in like manner: 28 questions and answers before starting engines; 5 as the engines were started; 2 before taxiing; 8 before takeoff; 4 after takeoff; 10 before landing; 15 after landing. The bombardiers had a checklist of 23 items before the engines were started and 11 as the airplane approached its bombing run. The navigator had a total of 19 points to check. The radio operator had 32. In the final analysis the airplane commander was responsible for the entire performance of his crew.

This transition from individual pilot to airplane commander marked the end of an era that had begun in World War I. The last vestiges of "the daring young man in the flying machine" finally disappeared. Gone were the black silk stocking fastened to the leather helmet and the white strip of parachute silk worn as a scarf. Gone were the jaunty leather coat and the boots and breeches that had lasted into the thirties. In their place was a very determined and rather serious young man in a prosaic cloth flying suit; his swagger stick had given way to a slide rule, and he carried a book of charts and diagrams which clearly showed that the art of seat-of-the-pants flying had changed to the science of computed flight control. The only carry-over was the battered and still jaunty fifty-mission cap.

The plane had an optimum set of manifold pressures, throttle settings, gross cowl flap settings, and rpm for every altitude airspeed; weight changed constantly with expenditure of fuel—and abruptly with release of bombs. Fuel load was carefully computed before takeoff, and since the margin of safety was kept as low as prudençe would permit, every effort had to be made to achieve maximum fuel efficiency.

A B-29 commander makes a final inspection of his crew before they take off from Guam in 1945 on the "Hirohito Highway" to Japan.

The manual which described the use of the "Composite Cruising Control Chart" contained an example which indicates the relationship of vital factors:

> *To find instrument air speed and power conditions for optimum attainment of a desired true cruising airspeed*
>
> Conditions (illustrative)
>
> Outside temperature—10° C
>
> Observed pressure altitude—10,000 ft.
>
> Gross weight (calculated)—90,000 lb.
>
> Desired true airspeed—292 mph
>
> Enter the curves at outside temperature: 10° C. Follow the projections and intersections through

Tons of bombs speckle the sky over Rangoon, Burma, as they spew from the yawning bomb bays of 20th Bomber Command Superfortresses based in India.

seven steps as illustrated and read:

RPM—2300
Manifold pressure—39 inches of mercury
Cowl flap gap—1 inch
Fuel consumption—775 gallons per hour
Instrument airspeed—253 mph

Computations and power settings were normally made and changed every two hours or with change of altitude.

Even the landing approach speed was computed in relation to the gross weight. The airplane was initially kept at about 160 mph with flaps at 25° in the approach pattern, and speed was decreased to a final approach at about 30 mph above computed power-off stalling speed for the existing gross weight.

The B-29 was reliable in her responses to power settings and control movements. But when she was straining to carry just as many bombs as possible under conditions of maximum performance, there was not too much room for error by the crew. In the early days of operation out of Saipan and Guam, before we had acquired an emergency landing field on Iwo Jima, some B-29s just didn't make it home from targets 1,500 miles away.

This scientific approach to flying large airplanes has become routine, but in 1944 it seemed unnatural—and somehow not quite in the right tra-

Admiral Nimitz, General Hansell, and Colonel Tibbetts inspecting a B-29 and crew.

dition for combat pilots who considered that their natural talents put them in a class apart.

The B-29 had a flying characteristic that was new to most of us. As soon as possible after takeoff it was necessary to get her "up-on-the-step" and flying slightly nose down till she reached 195 mph airspeed. You didn't go to a climb-out attitude immediately, as you could with a B-17. If you did, you simply mushed along at low speed consuming enormous quantities of gasoline. After reaching 195 you could climb all right, but after reaching cruising altitude it was again necessary to nose her down, get up on the step, and then set the controls for long-range cruise. This presented real problems if you were trying to maintain some sort of cruising formation.

It took a long time to learn to get maximum range from her. The final solution was very high manifold pressure coupled with very low rpm. This went counter to all our instincts. The big props were geared, and by the time you had cut engine rpm to the prescribed rate, you felt you could hear each labored cylinder explosion and count the propeller blades as they went by. To those of us who were accustomed to the smooth roar of high rpm it seemed unnatural and uncomfortable. But it cut fuel consumption way down.

On the last day of my crash course I went through another experience that stayed with me. We were flying over some very rugged terrain in New Mexico, a few thousand feet above the mountains. The instruction crew—who got pretty bored with these checkout rides—was engaged in a spirited game of gin rummy when one of them turned around, cut both throttles and mixtures on the right side, and feathered those props. He then went back to his gin rummy game. I struggled and worked myself into a lather. The control surfaces of the B-29 were large and didn't have much power-assist. Extreme left rudder could be held at the expense of a broken leg or a permanent malformation of the knee and ankle. Even with full power in the left engines I couldn't seem to hold altitude while I struggled to adjust trim tabs. After perhaps ten minutes, while I lost several thousand feet of altitude and several years of my life, the crew interrupted their game long enough to restore power on the right side. Yes, you could fly the B-29 with two engines out on the same side.

Like any fine steeplechase hunter the B-29 had a pace and cadence of her own, and the crew was well advised to observe it. You could roll easily and smoothly into a turn without excessive pressure on the controls, and she responded willingly without a break in stride. But if you tried to crowd her, to force her, she resisted and felt more like a Percheron on a beer wagon.

The engines overheated quickly on the ground. When we began operations in the tropical climate of Saipan we found that we could not afford the luxury of engine run-up and ignition check before takeoff. As a consequence we tested the engines and checked ignition on the actual takeoff run. A marker was placed along the runway, and if you were still having trouble by the time you reached it you cut the throttles and abandoned the takeoff. The engine characteristics were greatly improved with the later introduction of fuel injection.

When I took command of the Twenty-first Bomber Command, with headquarters at Peterson Field, Colorado Springs, we began simulated training attacks for the Mariana operations. We first had to adopt a standard formation and then laid out missions that were analogous to a run from

Saipan to Tokyo. Most of the B-29 groups were training on bases in Nebraska, Kansas, and Colorado; and we chose Havana, Cuba, as a representation of Tokyo. The first few missions were a ghastly disappointment to us. We hadn't learned the secrets of cruise control, and we wound up with airplanes down all over the southeastern part of the United States. This was in late August 1944. We had contracted to launch attacks from Saipan against Tokyo in November, yet we couldn't fly squadron formations the equivalent distance even *without bomb loads*—although we enjoyed all the benefits of weather information and communications and no enemy opposition. It was truly a shoestring operation that took off from Kansas for a still incomplete airstrip on Saipan. The 73rd Wing began the movement in October.

We had two mechanical difficulties that threatened disaster but were cleared up literally at the eleventh hour. The exhaust valves of the top rear cylinders were not getting enough cooling air and were burning out. This often caused engine fires, and the crankcases were cast magnesium which burned like a flare. This problem was finally solved by running in a gooseneck pipe which sprayed cool air directly on that valve housing, and putting cuffs on the props which pumped more air through the engine cowling. The other problem was frosting of panes in the cockpit and plastic bubbles at gunners' scanning stations. Wright Field found a cure for this by increasing the output of the heaters and running flexible hose lines to the panes of the cockpit windows and to the Plexiglas scanning bubbles. Fortunately there were no accidents resulting from frosting.

Toward the end of September I took the first B-29 to the Marianas. I joined one of the top crews of the 73rd Wing, and we started the flow which ultimately became massive. The crew was commanded by a very bright and capable young major named Jack Catton (who later became a four-star general, commanded the worldwide Military Airlift Command, and in 1973 was Commanding General Air Logistics Command). I'm sure he viewed my arrival with dismay, perhaps apprehension. I took a most unfair advantage of him by virtue of rank: I became the airplane commander and he the copilot. But if he had reservations and felt disappointment he concealed them well and accepted his temporary role with good grace.

We took off from Mather Field near Sacramento. The design gross weight of the B-29 was 120,000 pounds, but Wright Field reluctantly permitted an overload weight to 128,000. With our spare engine in the bomb bay and the various kits we carried, we weighed in at about 130,000 pounds. On the takeoff run I finally felt the weight lift from the landing gear and I made a cardinal mistake. I snubbed the brakes. This in itself was not bad; it was standard procedure after the wheels left the ground in order to stop their high-speed spinning as the gear was retracted. But when I hit the brakes we were not yet fully airborne. The braking action felt as if some giant hand had shoved us in the nose. Fortunately we got off all right, but we hugged the surface of the ground for a long time before we reached climbing speed. I don't know whether Jack Catton had been prematurely gray, but by the time he reached Saipan he was. If he had had time to look at me, he might have noticed a pale green cast of countenance.

On the leg from Honolulu to Kwajalein I swapped with Jack Catton, and he functioned as pilot. There was no snubbing of the brakes. But I was back in the left-hand seat, as we were about to start engines for the last leg of the trip to Saipan, when a young Navy lieutenant came up and

asked if we would lead him as far as Eniwetok, about 300 miles pretty much on our course. I made another mistake. I got a little flippant with the young man, asking him what kind of airplane he had; he replied with evident pride that he had a brand new Navy fighter. I asked him what speed he wanted to fly and assured him that we would be glad to slow down for him; we could easily make up the lost time after we had dropped him off. He told me, and I had to bend the throttles just a bit to make it, but I was feeling pretty smug when I called him on the radio to say that that was Eniwetok just ahead. His response was instantaneous: "OK, General. Sure appreciate this. Good luck. From here on you're on your own." He laughs best who laughs last.

The 73rd Wing was ready for takeoff on its first mission on 14 November, right on time. Engines were running with airplanes loaded to an illegal 140,000 pounds when a typhoon hit us and blotted out everything on the island. It was ten days before it was possible to undertake the mission, but on 23 November 1944, the Twenty-first Bomber Command attacked aircraft factories outside Tokyo and launched the beginning of what was soon to be the end.

The B-29, like the B-17 before her, had more staying power than her crews. Fifteen hours in the air in the face of a desperate enemy and plowing through terrible weather took its toll even of the magnificent crews. But they would never have been able to stick it out at all if they hadn't known they were riding the Grand National with a champion thoroughbred.

Although the B-29 was the latest of the very heavy bombers in World War II, the Convair XB-36 superbomber (right) illustrates the technological advancements of the AAF during the war. The B-29 had a wingspan of 141 feet, length of 99 feet, and range with bomb load of 4,100 miles; the XB-36 had a wingspan of 230 feet, length of 163 feet, and range with bomb load of 10,000 miles. The XB-36 was rolled out on 8 September, 1945 and first flew on 8 August 1946.

MAJ. GEN. HAYWOOD S. HANSELL, JR., was flying pursuit planes and bombers long before World War II. During the war he served as Commanding General of 3rd and then 1st Bomb Wing, 8th Air Force, and subsequently as Commanding General XXIst Bomber Command, 20th Air Force (B-29s) in 1944–45. He retired in 1946.

B-58 in flight.

B-58 Hustler

ROBERT E. HINNANT

AT Carswell Air Force Base in 1960 we were afforded regular views of the B-58 supersonic bomber, then being tested at the General Dynamics (GD) plant, which was across the runway used jointly by GD and the Air Force. The delta-winged Coke bottle fuselage, perched on long mosquito-legged tricycle landing gear without elevators, looked weird for a four-jet-engine nuclear bomber. Having B-47 and K-135 experience and having been assigned B-52s on base, I found the B-58 a completely different bomber; it had a sleek aggressive look, even with its long large pod hung under the belly to carry fuel and nuclear weapons or equivalent ballast.

It was no secret when the afterburners of the J-79 engines cut in that a B-58 was being flown by GD. Windows rattled and nerves were jangled for the 7,000–9,000-foot run on takeoff. I never really got used to the noise—just accepted it with earplugs or insulated earmuffs for the next nine years at three bases.

Finally the first aircraft went to the Air Force Test Force Group, and phase testing was completed. Aircraft were assigned to the 43rd Bomb Wing, were eventually declared combat ready, and went on to win the Strategic Air Command bombing competition within three weeks—an outstanding performance considering the seasoned B-47 and B-52 crews and aircraft competing as well as the crews and planes of the British Royal Air Force that participated in the competition under the same rules.

The B-58 operations began in 1958. Eight aircraft were configured as trainer-bombers in which the student pilot occupied the front seat, the instructor pilot the second, and the defense system operator (DSO) the third station. (The instructor pilot's seat was installed off-center so he could peek around the pilot during takeoff and landing.) A few hours in the trainer was all the pilot got before he was strapped into a bomber and waved off the ramp on his own. Many times the instructor who signed him off as qualified would run his beads through as he sat and sweated out the return and landing. Since the crews were handpicked with high standards, qualification solo flights were not a problem; the weak were weeded out before this phase of training.

We entered the three individual crew compartments from a stand that was rolled alongside the forward left side of the aircraft. In the first station was the pilot, in the second an observer (radar, navigator, bombardier), and in the third another observer (electronic countermeasures, remote fire control, and assistant to the pilot). The seats were open-jawed escape capsules, extremely complicated but 100 percent dependable. After checking the proper insertion of safety pins, we took our seats in the capsules. The first amazing realization was that the B-58 had a flight control *stick*, not a control column with a wheel. Secondly, we became aware that the cockpit was completely full—engine instruments, flight instruments, buttons, switches, lights, levers, throttles, and even a rearview mirror.

After stowing lunch, briefcase, and related papers we completed the electrical "power off" checklist; then the ground crew connected the external power and air conditioner, and the "before start" portion of the checklist was completed by the three crew members. A ground crew member, stationed in front of the aircraft on interphone, worked with the crew during aircraft systems checkout. When the three crew members agreed that the aircraft was satisfactorily configured for the particular mission, the aircraft commander (pilot) told the ground crew that he was ready to start engines. The "start engine" sequence was arranged so that aircraft electrical power and hydraulic (orinite) pressure output could be checked and used. The crew chief on the ramp determined that the engine air starter had properly disengaged, and the flight controls were checked visually by the ground crew in coordination with the pilot's movements of the stick and rudder. The B-58 had no fly-by-wire flight control systems or elevators. The elevons acted as aileron and elevator—a sophisticated system that gave the pilot the same feel all the time although control surface movement varied greatly during various flight conditions. When the external electrical power, air-for-start, and air conditioner were disconnected and another lengthy checklist completed by all three crew members, clearance for taxi was received from the control tower.

The above procedures were followed for routine training flights but were altered drastically when the aircraft was "cocked" on alert. In such a case the aircraft was configured for its specific wartime mission, normally with five atomic weapons, and a numbered crew assigned to a tail number aircraft. Under these conditions the complete alert force could be launched within five minutes from ground-alert posture. Practice "scrambles" from ground-alert posture were ordered by higher headquarters at random times and conditions, and the flight crews never knew whether or not it was the real thing until the appropriate code was given when ready for takeoff.

Taxi-out was simple and quick with nosewheel steering; the engines idled at about 72% rpm, gobbling fuel. Sharp turns were avoided when feasible, for the main landing gear had eight wheels each, small in size and inflated to approximately 265 psi with nitrogen (so a blown tire would not support combustion of any material). After aligning the aircraft on the runway and obtaining clearance from the control tower, the throttles were advanced, all instruments checked, then brakes released as power was advanced through afterburner cut-in.

The aircraft seemed to lunge forward as each engine contributed over 15,000 pounds of thrust. Computed takeoff data were used to check performance as the thousand-foot markers were passed; since takeoff airspeed, stopping distance, and three-engine performance were known, rapid

decisions had to be made until you passed the point on the runway where you were committed to go regardless. By then airspeed was around 190 knots; as the computed airspeed for takeoff was attained you rotated the aircraft positively, broke ground, and held attitude as a definite rate of climb was indicated and airspeed increased. At sea level the fully loaded B-58 climbed at a speed in excess of 17,000 feet per minute—a rate of climb that would have been creditable for a fighter of that day. When lightly loaded the Hustler shot upwards at 46,000 feet per minute, with afterburner! When the landing gear was retracted and "locked" indicated, airspeed was allowed to increase to climb speed; then you could listen to ground control or the bitch box and take a deep gulp of oxygen, check your flight plan, listen to the navigator or defense system operator (DSO), and become released from ground control.

Now it was simple if everything went according to plan. You put the

Control panel of B-58.

autopilot in the mode desired and followed your flight plan. If things were not operating normally, a female voice told you so (voice warning); if more than one malfunction occurred, the "old bitch" would tell you the most important one and would keep on until you did something about it. Of course warning lights flashed indicating malfunction; you could cover them up, but you couldn't stop the voice. The DSO was very helpful in reading various checklists, but the pilot took the actions or told the DSO to pull certain circuit breakers (he had hundreds in his compartment).

The B-58 responded to control stick and rudder movement very much as did the F-102, which was used for transition into the program because of its delta wing. When speed was increased through Mach 1 to Mach 2 or less, the center of gravity was shifted by either automatic or manual transfer of fuel into or out of the ballast tank located in the aft portion of the fuselage. This allowed the aircraft to ride on the downhill slope of the sonic air crest. Also, as speed increased the spikes or center cones in each engine inlet had to extend so that the sonic shock wave never entered the engine, now that the speed was limited by maximum allowable inlet air temperature and by structural factors. The aircraft was *not* power limited. Normal speed for cruise was over 525 knots (Mach .92), over 600 knots at sea level, and 1,147 knots above 40,000 feet. The B-58 has been flown above 85,000 feet with a payload.

The four engines were the J-79-5B General Electric axial type with afterburner. The sea level static ratings were: maximum power with after-

B-58 Hustler taking off.

burner—15,500 pounds thrust at 7,734 rpm maximum continuous for 120 minutes; military power—10,300 pounds thrust at 7,460 rpm continuous. Normal cruise was 9,700 pounds thrust continuous with a maximum allowable exhaust gas temperature of 1,105°F under all conditions.

Air refueling from a KC-135 tanker was easy compared to other air-refueled receivers. The A/R receptacle was aft of the crew compartments atop the fuselage; when flying within the refueling "envelope" you were below the jet wash of the KC-135, with the directional lights on the belly of the tanker right in your face. On refueling to full tanks, it was best to put the two outboard engines in afterburner, then adjust power on the inboard engines to maintain position. The dependable KC-135 tanker with proficient crew was a welcome sight, for the rendezvous was accomplished many times over midocean or polar ice cap. Range with one refueling was 7,400 nautical miles; without refueling, 4,450 miles.

There were two types of pod carried under the belly. The MB-1 type was a single unit in which fuel and nuclear weapon/ballast were carried; some contained photo equipment. The two-component pod carried fuel in the lower section, which could be jettisoned after the fuel was used; the upper component contained the warhead. Four smaller nuclear weapons could be carried externally, two on each side, between the inboard engines and the fuselage, one behind the other. When the B-58 was configured for combat, it was loaded with five atomic weapons; thus five separate targets could be hit at either low or high level. Exit from the target area was made by a zoom to maximum altitude at Mach 2 or to low level at Mach .92. The electronic countermeasure (ECM) equipment was superior in all respects, and the bomb/navigation equipment provided accurate delivery of high-yield weapons.

After penetration, escape from defended areas was enhanced by the B-58's high speed, small size and minimum radar reflectivity, radar warning systems, defensive ECM systems, and tail turret. When all else failed, you could "punch out" in the capsule with a supply of oxygen, signal for directional finders, and dispense chaff for radar tracking. Parachutes opened automatically and let you down gently; if in water, the flotation gear inflated. You had with you a full survival kit including radio, flares, gun, food, water, clothing, and even sunburn lotion and fishing kit!

At the termination of a mission, a normal jet penetration was made from a known beacon to the airfield; usually the Aircraft Control ground unit would direct you for the approach to the runway, and Ground Control Approach would pick you up and complete the circuit to the runway. Both Instrument Landing System (ILS) and Tactical Air Navigation (TACAN) were installed in all aircraft and usually worked well. After computing the best approach speed, which varied with aircraft weight, you flew that speed until you bled off airspeed to computed best flare speed for touchdown. You could not add a few knots speed for your wife and one for each child and still stop on the runway, even though a brake chute was used. You flew the speed and rate of descent exactly, and your attitude was 16° nose high. Just adding power, nose high, would not hack a decrease in descent rate. The nose had to come down to streamline the aircraft before airspeed increased and rate of descent decreased. This may sound odd to some, but the delta wing has that trait. On the runway, on the proper heading, you pulled the brake chute at 160 knots or below and raised the nose high to get aerodynamic braking with the lower wing surface. The brake chute shear pin would shear at above 160 knots—a safety feature in case a go-around was attempted after deploying the chute. At normal landing, ground roll of 2,580 feet was required.

After turning off the runway, completing the after-landing checklists, parking, and shutting down, you unstrapped yourself from the aircraft, installed the three ground safety pins in the capsule, and were helped to unfold and climb out onto the entrance stand. You then walked around the aircraft before going to maintenance and operations debriefing. We were usually numb, so questions were answered with a shrug, a nod, or sometimes a recitation concerning the complete outfit with name-calling; after 45 minutes we were turned loose to make our way home to hear what really happened today—from our families.

Overall the B-58 handled and performed beautifully. The utmost skill was used in the application of miniaturized automatic solid-state components, exotic metals, plastics, rubber, grease, and orinite to make the aircraft exceed its design specifications. It was expensive to fly (dollars per flying hour), but that's progress, I guess. The aircraft seemed to have their own personalities for some crews, especially some tail-numbered dogs or jewels. Most crew members were especially proud of the airplane. Even though those in the second and third stations only had a 4 × 6-inch window to look through, claustrophobia never seemed to cause a problem, for you were too busy to look. The tandem seating arrangement required close crew coordination and cooperation at all times, especially during malfunction and high-speed flight. Most crews were gung ho, like that of N. R. Smith (later killed in Vietnam on his second mission in an O-2): when he came out after weather briefing to board the aircraft, a panel was yet to be installed after a discrepancy had been discovered on preflight. He told the crew chief, "If you want that panel to have as much flight time as the airframe, you'd better screw it on quick—I'm going." Prior flight experience in B-47s was a real asset, as was delta-wing fighter time.

The B-58—fast, complicated, computerized, and not power limited—ranked above the B-47 and B-52. Detailed knowledge of the aircraft systems and thorough flight planning were necessary, and takeoff time was scheduled well in advance. The two observers in the B-58 had two or three aeronautical ratings, and the aircraft commander (pilot) was usually triple-rated. In the B-47 there was a copilot who could fly the aircraft, operate the tail guns, act as radio operator, and serve coffee or water when necessary. In the B-58 the crew members were on their own in separate stalls, and everyone had his separate duties. You could stand and stretch your legs in the B-47; the B-52—with its two pilots, two or three observers, and tail gunner—gave some freedom of movement and relief from duties at odd intervals; not so in the B-58.

Everything was not always smooth flying in the B-58. The bombing-navigation system would act up (even though there were nine modes of bombing); and there were flight control malfunctions, engine problems, and wheel and tire explosions. During the cold weather test in Alaska an aircraft skidded sideways, and three of the four engines flamed out. The second-station operator asked on interphone what was going on and where they were; there was no answer, for the pilot was giving all his attention to keeping the aircraft in the air, straightening it out, and getting some engines running again. The navigator, second station, kept asking where they were but received no response. Since the airspeed and altitude were going to pot he decided to "punch out." By the time the pilot had started another engine and landed safely, a rescue helicopter had picked up the navigator and deposited him on the ramp. When the haggard pilot crawled out of the aircraft, the navigator rushed over, stuck his face within inches of the pilot's, and demanded, "Why didn't you tell me where we were? I am the navigator and have a right to know!"

To again illustrate the caliber of crew and aircraft, another incident is noteworthy. A "roll cloud" was in the vicinity of Bunker Hill Air Force Base, and the weather was bad. The pilot was cleared for an approach, but as he was descending on the glide path he entered the roll cloud and was forced down by the draft. He applied power but was not able to avoid a high commercial power line, which sheared the control cables to No. 3 and No. 4 engines. The landing gear snagged a chain link fence and dragged about 30 feet of it as they proceeded to the alternate and landed safely. This was a determined crew and a good airplane.

Many other interesting accomplishments are known, but none of the B-58s now stored at Tucson, Arizona, is likely ever to fly again. It was an extremely formidable deterrent weapons system; although it never had to perform its mission, it did its job by being ready for eight years.

Nine of COL. ROBERT E. HINNANT'S 21 years with Strategic Air Command were spent with B-58s, primarily in a support capacity—supply, maintenance, inspections, retrofit, and modifications of the weapons system. He retired after 28 years of active duty.

C-46 Commando over the first ridge of the Hump en route to China, 1944.

C-46 Commando

WILLIAM S. WOZNEK

THE 58th Squadron of the 375th Troop Carrier Group flew C-47s under adverse conditions in the battle for the Pacific during World War II. We had moved from Port Moresby to Dobodura to Nadzab and now we were on Biak Island, Dutch New Guinea. The C-47 Skytrain had served us faithfully in our missions to advance bases over enemy-held positions. Our cargo included almost anything that could be moved through the large cargo doors—from pigeons and silverware to observation planes, prefabricated outhouses, jeeps, troops, bombs, gasoline, and miscellaneous supplies. Sometimes the supplies were dropped, but usually we landed on quickly improvised landing strips cut from the jungle. Unfortunately some of the return trips included both wounded and dead troops.

The 2nd Combat Cargo Group joined us on Biak. Our roles were the same even if our names seemed to indicate a difference. We flew the same kinds of cargo to and from the same jungle flight strips; the difference was in the aircraft we flew. Theirs were the new and much larger C-46 Curtiss Commandos.

We had grown to know our C-47s like a comfortable pair of old shoes, and some of us owed our lives to the aircraft's capabilities in times of stress. Many of us were saddened by the news that the 47 was being replaced by the 46—a beast of unknown quality and questionable reputation. But it was inevitable, and in December 1944 another flight commander and I were assigned to a crew and plane from the 2nd Combat Cargo Group for a flight check prior to delivery of new C-46 aircraft to the 375th Group.

The passing of almost thirty years has faded the finite technicalities, but the gross impressions remain. The transition in size seemed greater from C-47 to C-46 than had been the move from trainer to C-47. The engines appeared to be massive but in proportion to their four-bladed props. The Boeing Stratocruiser type of double fuselage could be entered only with a ladder—a task which awed some who entered for the first time.

Those of us who had been fortunate enough to have flown the AT-9 found a familiar cockpit arrangement. Both planes had been built by Curtiss, and it appeared that the very functional cockpit of the AT-9 had been transposed to the C-46. This familiarity proved to be an asset, since no handbooks were available or briefings provided before our first and only transition flight. The check pilot seemed a bit embarrassed at having to check ride individuals whose overseas time and combat experience were so much greater than his own. His teaching technique was to answer questions; if no questions were asked, no information was volunteered.

A brief familiarization with the controls and switches and their operation was followed by starting both engines and taxiing to the flight strip. It was fortunate that the wind was calm, because the massive fin and rudder provided a surface that in a strong wind turned the plane into a weathervane. The use of throttle to taxi seemed to add to taxi speed without sufficient directional control—a situation which made reliable brakes a necessity not always available. Brake systems on the C-46 seemed adequate only when new, and "new" appeared to be for only the first day of use, with the result that one always assumed that brakes were at the point of failure. The problem was exaggerated because the brakes never seemed to work evenly, and frequent loss of hydraulic fluid could be anticipated.

The transition training lasted a total of two hours. We each did two touch-and-go landings and an engine-out procedure. We were now considered qualified C-46 pilots, expected to provide training and experience for other flight commanders and the pilots and copilots in our individual flights. To say that we were ill-equipped for the task would be a gross understatement, and the difficulty was compounded by the lack of an airplane for training purposes.

It was January 1945, more than a month since our first and only flight in the C-46, when we were assigned our first aircraft. Supplies were needed in the Philippines, and here was a perfect opportunity for on-the-job training. A bit of cockpit time would have been desirable, but we had to be off if we were to meet any kind of schedule. Fortunately the crew chief was familiar with starting procedures, and with his help we got under way. I am sure he would have preferred to abandon ship at the revetment. The radio operator was muttering with a grim look and clenched teeth. The copilot at this point was little more than an observer, since this was his first experience with the Commando. (The name was indeed impressive!)

We were cleared for takeoff and started our roll. The initial acceleration seemed a bit ponderous, but the roar of the 4,000 horsepower was reassuring as the airspeed indicator needle climbed slowly. The hydraulic boost control system had little palpable effect on the plane's flight characteristics, and the plane did not appear to be hasty about becoming airborne. A little more nose-up trim was added as we entered the last fourth of a 4,000-foot strip.

Biak is less than a hundred miles from the equator, and the sun beat down on the coral strip and the lumbering C-46. I could feel the strained presence of the crew chief standing between the pilot seats. The copilot was puzzled that this powerful machine was not airborne as quickly as a 47. Back pressure was gently applied and increased. It wanted to fly—it better fly—we were approaching the end of the strip. A bit more back pressure and it came off the ground, not much more than a couple of hundred feet from the end of the runway.

Fortunately we did not need to gain altitude rapidly. After liftoff the plane went into malarian chills as it shook and shuddered until it

A C-46 accompanied in flight by a P-40.

seemed every rivet would pop and all the instruments would fall out. The control column trembled as if possessed by some native witch doctor. This I assumed to be the indication of a power-on stall and quickly called for "gear up" as I dropped the nose slightly to assume nearly level flight. The symptoms disappeared.

Three months of squadron operations passed without incident, but there was a common complaint that the airplane did not want to fly in a loaded configuration. Each of us experienced stall tendencies on takeoff, and we wondered about our operating procedures. Weight and balance on the C-47 were no problem—load about 5,000 pounds and keep it well forward. The same procedure was used on the C-46, only the figure was 10,000 pounds.

We decided to recheck our information that the C-46 would carry 10,000 pounds, and we found that the original information was correct but the interpretation was different. We had been operating on the basis of weight loaded into the cabin, without including the normal operating elements of full tanks, crew, and auxiliary rescue equipment. The results had been that under ideal conditions we were operating with a 2,000-pound overload off short strips at tropical temperatures. This news gave us new respect for the airplane, and a change in loading weights improved flight characteristics remarkably.

Landing at full gross weight was not recommended, but we often wondered about the possible consequences should the occasion arise. The Commando proved, at least in one instance, to be equal to the task. We had a full load of fuel in the tanks, a complete airborne 6 x 6 truck, two passengers, and miscellaneous cargo on board. The estimated weight of the cargo was 11,500 pounds, which was 1,500–3,300 pounds over our normal load.

Everything was checked, and the takeoff roll and liftoff with the now-accepted stall vibration were normal. The copilot was given the "gear up" signal as we crossed the end of the strip. Almost simultaneously a resounding explosion was heard from the starboard engine, and it immediately began to shake in sympathy with the rest of the airplane. There was a loss of rpm and manifold pressure but no other indication of our problem.

I could hear the crew chief almost screaming in my ear, "Feather it! Feather it!" I didn't believe the plane would stay in the air with only one engine with our load, and I could visualize the 6 x 6 coming through the cockpit in a forced landing. We decided to utilize what power we had, hoping that the vibration would not tear the engine from its mount and possibly take the wing with it, and try to land.

We leveled off at 200 feet and started a gentle left turn over the water. The tower was notified of our problem, and we were cleared for landing. Fire equipment was moved to the strip and a harbor unit was alerted for a possible water landing. Nearly maximum power was used on the good engine, and only enough power to maintain our speed and altitude was demanded of the ailing engine in order to minimize the vibration. I am positive we could not have survived in this overloaded configuration had the starboard engine been feathered. I must hasten to mention that the C-46 would perform exceptionally well with a full legal load on a single engine.

The pattern was unorthodox, but we managed a good approach leg to the strip. If there was ever to be a good landing, this had to be it. The combination of our gross weight and a hard landing brought visions of the landing gear struts protruding through the wing.

The low altitude gave little time to trim the plane after closing the throttles. Touchdown at the beginning of the strip seemed imperative, since I wasn't too happy about stopping the momentum of this load and judged the prospects of a controlled ground loop and its effects on the gear.

Touchdown was at the very near end of the strip and feather light. The coral pebbles began to turn the wheels before the shocks took up the weight of the aircraft. Deceleration without brakes was such that power was necessary to taxi to the far end of the strip. The color began to come back into our cheeks by the time we had returned the plane to its repair area, where close examination indicated a blown cylinder in the starboard engine.

Many more incidents could be mentioned as to the marvelous capabilities of this aircraft, but it continued to have a bad image, especially on single engine. A visiting civilian factory representative appeared deathly afraid of the airplane. He would not relinquish the left seat in a flight demonstration and permitted us to fly only momentarily from the right seat. When asked to demonstrate a full-feathered single-engine landing, he refused. When asked to observe my procedures for a full-feathered single-engine landing, he said he would watch from the ground.

In my opinion, the C-46 had the potential to become a great airplane. The mechanical deficiencies were a result of hurried production for a wartime effort, exaggerated by the experiences of inadequately prepared crews. C-46 casualties were emphasized, but there was no mention that they were often caused by tremendously exceeding the operational limits. It is unfortunate that the Commando was replaced by more modern cargo aircraft before it had the recognition it truly deserved.

DR. WILLIAM S. WOZNEK is associate professor of education at Bloomsburg State College, Pennsylvania. His flying career began in 1938 at age sixteen, and he spent more than two years flying troop carrier missions in the Southwest Pacific Theater during World War II.

C-47 transport takes off from a base in India en route to Burma during a driving monsoon rain. Note circles of moisture outlining the arc of the propeller blades.

C-47 Dakota *and* AC-47

ROBIN HIGHAM
JAMES L. COLE, JR.

THE first time I was really impressed by a Dakota was in 1945 when we were taxiing around Kemble, England, in an Oxford and passed a C-47 standing next to a Halifax. I was surprised to find that the Dakota appeared to be much bigger than one of RAF Bomber Command's heavy bombers. What made the Dakota so impressive was the round fuselage compared to the slim rectangular one on the Halifax; otherwise their dimensions were about the same, though the Halifax had four engines and the Dakota only two.

On the ground the Dakota had a tendency to look massive from the tail because of the great fin and rudder and elevators and the size of the fuselage; from the nose it looked like a dainty bird with a clean rounded beak, compared to the cluttered noses of most contemporary multiengine military machines with their guns and the like. Like all pretricycle-gear aircraft the Dakota stood high off the ground so that the cockpit towered above a spectator. Today of course a DC-3 (the civilian C-47) looks like a puppy following a mother 707 around O'Hare.

The impression of size was further accentuated for the novice when he first climbed into the rear end of the cabin, walked a long distance up the cabin toward the cockpit, opened the door, went past the navigator's table and the outside cockpit door (both on the left side), and finally entered the cockpit. From here he looked down about 25 feet to the ground. Moreover, for one just out of an Oxford (as I was) the wingspan seemed enormous; there was as much wing on one side as the whole span of the Oxford. Neither pilot could see the wing on the opposite side of the aircraft, which made taxiing alone very dicey—in fact, in the RAF it was forbidden. The constant fear of getting a black mark for an accident made us especially careful, for in 1945 no one wanted to be thrown off flying. Size was further accentuated in the air where—although the C-47 was a very docile aircraft—its stall, which was at first ponderous and hard to achieve, was an abrupt and sudden dropping of the nose with a sinking feeling. But recovery was

C-47 in flight.

quickly achieved with some power and use of the great tail surfaces. The other result of size was the poor rate of roll with the ailerons, since they were very long and narrow. Thus while pitching and skidding were easily achieved, turns were rather gentle if done smoothly with the needle and ball properly centered.

Before a flight the copilot circled the machine, inspecting the controls and seeing that the wooden wedges that locked the three movable surfaces were removed. If there was much of a wind, we sometimes instructed the ground crew to leave the locks in until after the engines were started, in order to prevent flapping and to ease the strain on the pilots until George (the automatic pilot) could be engaged. This practice was frowned on by authorities, and quite properly, since the CO of the Transport Command Conversion Unit was killed shortly before I joined the unit when trying to take off with the locks in. He had also failed to follow instructions to check the controls manually and visually before takeoff, to make sure they were free. Preflight inspection included the oleo legs, tires, and fuel drain cocks, which were to be wired shut. The copilot also instructed the ground crew to pull the pins from the undercarriage legs once the engines were running and the captain gave the signal. These pins were ¼-inch affairs dropped into a hole behind each undercarriage leg to prevent the undercarriage from collapsing while the aircraft was without hydraulic pressure. After the engines were started and pressure had reached 825–875 pounds, the captain would hold up his left hand with the thumb and forefinger making a circle and then withdraw the index finger of the right hand from it. In the RAF where P/O Prune was the captain who could never get his finger out and so get promoted to F/O (Flying-Officer), this was usually a ribald signal, generally answered by the ground crew with an earthy rendition of Churchill's V for Victory signal of two fingers waved upwards. Once removed, the pins were handed to the wireless operator at the back door, who brought them to the cockpit, reported, and stowed them away.

Before starting the engines the pilot and copilot would run through the cockpit drill: intercom on, generator on, brakes on (even though the aircraft was against chocks), master switch off, George off, and cross-feed off. The battery switch was then set to "on" and fuel placed on "main tanks" and checked for fullness, since we never flew without full tanks if we could help it, especially over Burma. Next the throttles were opened one inch; the mixture set to "idle-cut out," propeller pitch to "fine," carburetor heat to "cold" (or on the MKIV to "ram"); the gills opened; and the master and individual ignition switches turned on. If the copilot was starting the engines, he usually started the starboard one first. This meant setting the starboard booster pump switch to "on" (or pumping the wobble pump on earlier models) and then switching on the energizer. Immediately there was a high whine, and the propeller would slowly begin to turn over. If all went well, it would begin to accelerate after a number of loud bangs, splutters, and a cloud of smoke from the exhaust pipe. If it did not catch in 30 seconds, the energizer had to be rested and another attempt made. When both engines were running, the battery cart would be waved away and the aircraft allowed to start warming up at 800–1,000 rpm. While temperatures were climbing to 40° C for the oil and 120° C for cylinder heads, a cockpit check was made, flaps tested on both hydraulic systems, and the blind-flying panel set up. On the MKIV, which was fitted with supercharged engines, the blower controls were moved at 1,200 rpm from low to high

C-47s towing gliders to Normandy coast on D day, 6 June 1944.

and back to low while the momentary drop in oil pressure was observed to make sure they were functioning.

An experienced pilot anxious to get off the ground would now wave away the chocks, look around to see if any unwary friends were in a position to have their caps blown off as he left the area, open up the throttles, and trust that the journey around the taxi track would give the engines time enough to warm up. Eager or experienced crews would then start the takeoff check—running the engines up to 25 inches, exercising the pitch mechanism, moving the mixture control to lean until the revs dropped, even opening up to 30 inches on both engines against the brakes and then pulling back to 650–800 rpm to check slow running. In Burma we rarely had troubles with cold engines after the first start in the morning. Nor was overheating a great problem, even though we were once held on the ground at Akyab for 15 minutes by a nervous controller who had a Mosquito coming in.

The actual takeoff check was the RAF's standard mnemonic HTMPFFGG: Hydraulics (825–875 pounds); Trim to neutral and tighten throttle damping nut; Mixture to auto-rich, carburetor heat to cold, and adjust oil cooler shutters; Pitch to fully fine; Fuel on and check contents again of all four tanks; Flaps up; Gills to trail; set Gyros. Then open engines once to clear the plugs of oil from idling, and lock tail wheel after the aircraft is lined up on the runway.

Takeoff itself was not difficult with the great rudder available. Throttles were advanced to between 35 and 47 inches of boost, depending on the load. The copilot now did strapped-in contortions, his right hand keeping the throttles forward and his left down beside his seat on the gear lever. Normally we got the tail up as soon as possible, let her gain speed, and then lifted off at about 80 mph indicated. Our favorite ploy at this point was to climb about 30 feet and then put the nose down and aim for the end of the runway. This allowed a rapid buildup of airspeed and a satisfying whoom up into the air at the boundary fence before settling into a steady climb at 125 mph. Takeoff boost and rpm were then reduced in stages starting at 500 feet. Upon reaching altitude, boost was generally reduced to about 27 inches and rpm to 1,850, though we normally aimed for 165 mph on the clock and adjusted boost and rpm upwards to achieve this. Since we nearly always flew with a full 5,500 pounds in the cabin and occasionally—with erratic weighing machines—up to 8,000, it took more power than the manual specified on operations.

When heavily loaded, the Dakota had a tendency to wallow. This happened to us particularly after a heavily loaded takeoff from Don Maung, Bangkok, with only 1,000 yards of runway available. As we thundered down the open half of the runway, she just was not getting off. We eventually dumped full flap at 950 yards and barely cleared the Japanese working party relaying the other half of the runway. We knew we were way over the 26,500-pound landing weight so could not turn back; we gradually staggered up in the hot air until, as it grew cooler higher up, the controls got firmer. But for an hour or so she still felt mushy.

Landing after a couple of hours of flight even with a full load was not so bad. We slid down into the circuit and on the downwind leg reduced speed to 130, lowered the undercarriage, pushed the mixture to auto-rich, checked the gills on trail, increased pitch to 2,400 rpm, checked fuel, and lowered one-quarter flaps. After turning on final and reducing to 120 mph,

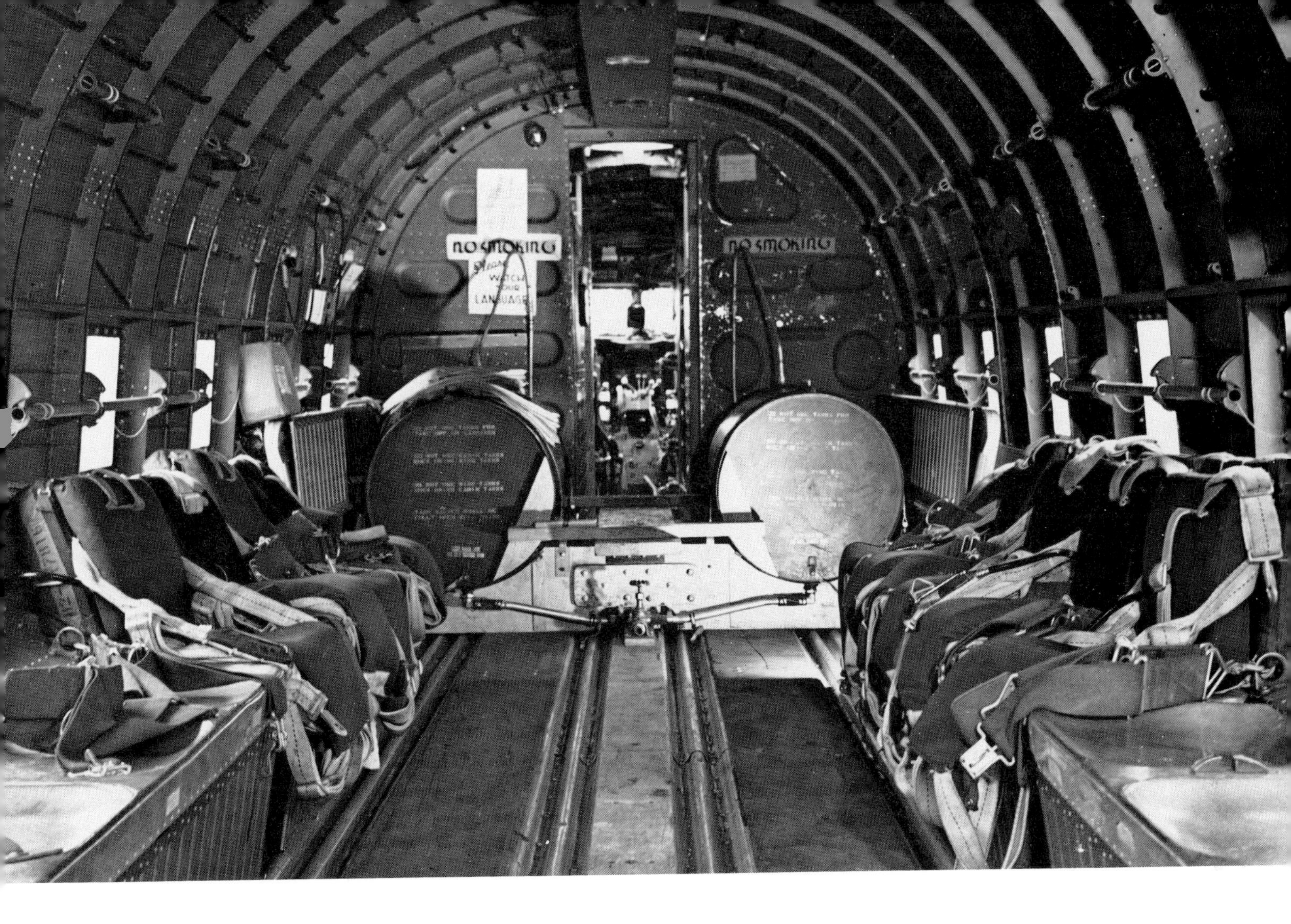

with full flaps and fine pitch (a maneuver that at night we usually managed to do right over the village in the middle of the approach path at Conversion Unit), we settled down to a normal engine-assisted approach at 95 mph or a glide at 105 or a single-engine approach at 110. Touchdown was on the main wheels if fully loaded; three-point landings were permissible and encouraged, though there was a tendency for the light aircraft to bounce unless handled carefully. We once landed back at base with several spare crews as passengers; when the unfortunate skipper bounced it, the cabin rang to "One!" "Two!" "Three!" The brakes are described in the manual as "fierce"; "good" would be a better word. Unlike British brakes of the day, they were reliable toe-operated hydraulic ones and brought the aircraft to a quick, smooth stop. We landed once at Chittagong, India, in 220 yards.

Interior of C-47. This aircraft is fitted with special internal tankage and parachutes. RAF crews usually did not wear chutes in Dakotas.

Dakotas were used extensively with airborne forces. This meant special kinds of flying. For paratroop work we flew in a close formation stepped up one behind the other, so that men dropping out of the leading aircraft would not smash into those behind and below—a lesson, we always heard, that had been learned the hard way. Quick anticipatory use of the controls was required in flying close formation, since it was very easy with that big rudder and small nose as a reference for a Dakota to get into a pendulum action skidding from side to side of the aircraft in front. Once mastered, a tight formation was a lot of fun; one of the games was to see if you could bump the top of the rudder of the plane ahead with your nose. For the actual paratroop dropping, speed was reduced to 90 mph with partial flaps, altitude about 600 feet.

Glider towing was another matter. The gliders were marshaled alongside the runway in use. Towropes were laid out on the ground. The C-47 tug taxied onto the runway and moved slowly ahead until signaled to stop by the marshaler. Then the end of the towrope was shoved up an orifice in the tail until it snap-locked. The copilot hastily checked that he was in communication on the intercom with the glider, and the marshaler waved the aircraft slowly forward until the 200-foot towrope lifted off the ground, whereupon he signaled all clear for takeoff. The Dakota pilot then opened up his throttles smoothly and fully, while the poor copilot twisted in his seat with his right hand backing up the throttles and his left over his shoulder holding the towrope release handle. The tug advanced, with much groaning, trying to keep as straight as possible. Usually the glider became airborne first, and it was at this point that the copilot's left hand could get itchy. If the glider failed to skim the runway and rose instead into the air, it would pull the tail of the tug up so that the tug could get no lift. If this happened, the copilot was supposed to shout a warning and pull the towrope release handle. This was not a popular move, both because it meant a time-wasting abortive launching and more particularly because if the glider pilot did not pull the release at his end first, 200 feet of elasticized nylon rope with a substantial metal fitting on the end could come zinging back through the Perspex of the cockpit and decapitate the glider crew.

If all went well on takeoff, the glider rose slightly above the tug, being careful again not to stall him, and rode just above the slipstream. The tug pilots anxiously watched oil and cylinder head temperatures and reduced power as soon as they could. Once past 1,000 feet, both ends of the towrope could relax. A slow further climb would continue, as pilots watched carefully for the other elements of the glider stream as well as for rival ones. Once at cruising altitude, a glider with an experienced crew was no problem for the tug, though the aircraft still had to be flown manually. Fuel consumption was higher and speed lower than normal.

Arriving in the vicinity of the landing zone, the Dakota crew gave the glider crew a fix and a countdown to cast off. Once the glider left, the tug accelerated and tended to climb. The trailing towrope was eventually jettisoned at a recovery point or simply abandoned to black marketeers. The rest of the trip was flying a light aircraft home.

One peculiar problem we encountered one day was that our aircraft had an inexplicable tendency suddenly to start sliding toward another Dakota we were trying to photograph. This meant a hasty abandonment of cameras, both pilots on the wheel, shoving the nose down, and diving under the other machine. Once down behind, the aircraft would return to normal. It was not until I went back to the toilet that I discovered what was happening. We were carrying a load of Sikhs who did not speak English and who had not flown before. Apparently, whenever the other aircraft became visible, they undid their seat belts and went across to the other side of the aircraft to watch it. Most upsetting, but luckily not disastrous.

The Dakota was a joy to fly because of its general reliability. We had a slow flight from England to Chittagong—losing the high-speed blower on one engine right after takeoff from Down Ampney, having to replace both engines at El Adem, and two other maintenance problems—resulting in 28 days en route. But out of Chittagong we flew the two jinx aircraft of the squadron's twenty-eight; the only time we had trouble in the air was when a battery boiled over while climbing away from base, causing us to return and make a gingerly landing at maximum weight. Given a choice, I would fly the "Gooney Bird" again without qualms.

DR. ROBIN HIGHAM is professor of history at Kansas State University and the editor of *Aerospace Historian*. His service in World War II was with the RAF.

AN airplane is a mechanical creation that is as a rule obsolescent, eventually becoming obsolete. In most cases it simply wears out and breaks down. The ubiquitous C-47, however, has proved to be an exception to this general rule. The aging but apparently ageless "Gooney Bird" is still a consistent and reliable performer, and its durability and versatility keep it in constant demand. For years the C-47 was known worldwide as a superlative military transport aircraft. Some 10,123 of them were manufactured by Douglas, and the aircraft was absolutely indispensable to the Allied war effort during World War II as well as to our own air effort in the Korean conflict. However, larger and faster military transport aircraft began to replace the war-weary C-47s, especially after Korea, and civilian airlines also sought new and faster models to replace their DC-3s. The Air Force began to consider the C-47 obsolete and the airlines considered the DC-3 outmoded, although they did not abandon them entirely.

The air war in Indochina, however, gave the "Gooney Bird" a new lease on life. The tactical requirements of the Vietnam War spawned the AC-47, a truly singular weapons system in the history of airpower. At first many were doubtful that the ancient transport could function effectively as an attack aircraft, but the C-47 was to prove most worthy of the new prefix on its designation.

As a brash young lieutenant I was somewhat amused by the specter of an old C-47 plunging into combat sporting three 7.62 mm Gatling-type miniguns, but my amusement changed to intense interest when I received orders for Vietnam and the 4th Air Commando Squadron (AC-47). During combat crew training the C-47 proceeded to educate me, as it had hundreds of lieutenants for many years, in the techniques of the tail wheel and its unique solution to the problem of crosswind landings. Like others I gained tremendous respect for the airplane as a flying machine, and in addition the gunnery problem proved to be fascinating. The side-firing guns of the AC-47 could be installed with anywhere from 0° to 18° declination from the lateral axis of the aircraft. This gave necessary flexibility, for the desired amount of declination depended primarily on the altitude of the aircraft, in turn dictated by the mission and the tactical environment in which the aircraft was operating. At operational altitudes near 1,500 feet, for example, 0° declination was ideal; as the altitude was increased, the degree of declination would be increased to reduce the bank angle and amount of cross-controlling required to track a target. Consequently the AC-47 with appropriate gun declination was found to be extremely effective at just about any altitude.

In the unconventional warfare environment of Vietnam a firing altitude of 3,000 feet above the ground and a gun declination of 12° proved to be ideal; the aircraft was above the effective range of small arms, yet bullets from the aircraft struck the ground target with an impact velocity of 812 feet per second—more than sufficient to kill troops in the open. The guns were thus mounted in the aircraft at a 12° angle, although this could be altered by maintenance crews if aircraft were deployed to a different operating environment.

The actual act of firing was accomplished with the aircraft in a modified left pylon turn on the intended target; proper slant range, airspeed, altitude, bank angle, and roll-in point guaranteed accurate ordnance delivery. These are difficult conditions to meet simultaneously, and success depended on the handling characteristics of the aircraft and the skill of the pilot. The smooth flight characteristics, general airworthiness, and control responsiveness of the reliable C-47 were significant factors in successful target acquisition, tracking, sighting, and firing.

The AC-47's primary mission was night close support. Carrying 21,000 rounds of 7.62 mm ammunition and 45 Mark 24 illumination flares, the aircraft was a self-contained weapons system that combined the attributes of devastating firepower and extended loiter capability.

"Puff the Magic Dragon" or "Spooky," as the aircraft came to be known, performed a variety of other missions as well. In addition to providing firepower and flare support for field forces and outposts, squadron pilots also functioned in a forward air controller capacity by directing jet fighter strikes. The 4th Air Commando Squadron AC-47s also attacked roads, canals, supply trails, and enemy camps as well as flying search and rescue assignments and even hauling cargo.

The reliability and durability of the C-47, its age notwithstanding, made it the ideal aircraft for such diversified operations. During its first year of combat operations the 4th Air Commando Squadron flew 22,752 combat sorties and fired over 12 million rounds of ammunition. The squadron was awarded the Air Force Outstanding Unit Award for the period from 1 November 1965 to 9 March 1966; the citation accompanying the award indicated that the ancient "Gooney Bird" deserved the honor as

AC-47 in flight over Vietnam, 1967. Note cannon poking out of the window forward of the main door.

much as the aircrews. It stated that "the personnel of this squadron used the same aircraft for airlifting people and cargo, armed reconnaissance, forward air controlling, and for testing new counterinsurgency concepts." Even the wildest dreamer could not have imagined that the ancient transport, born in the days of wooden propellers and open cockpits, would become a potent strike aircraft in an age of supersonic jet fighters.

The character of the war in Vietnam underwent a significant change as large units of battalion and regimental strength were encountered, well armed with heavy weapons and more than willing to stand and fight. The conflict became in many ways a conventional or limited war rather than strictly a contest of insurgents and counterinsurgents. We aircrew members were painfully aware that the AC-47 was hardly designed to engage in such warfare, but if the AC-47 was not intended for such action no one would have guessed it in the light of subsequent events.

On the night of 5 September 1967, a force of 1,200 Viet Cong launched an attack on Tam Ky, the capital city of Quang Tin Province. Three AC-47s—commanded by Major R. H. Anderson, 1st Lieutenant C. T. Hill, and myself—were summoned to assist the South Vietnamese forces defending the city. The ensuing struggle was as wearisome as it was violent. A C-130 flareship operating above us added a thorny complication to our Dragonships' on-target operations. The ground forces needed as much illumination as possible, and the C-130 kept the sky filled with Mark 24 flares. In addition to silhouetting the Dragonships for the Viet Cong gunners, the flares constituted a formidable flight hazard for the AC-47s. We were forced to subject the aircraft to much violent "yanking and banking" to avoid colliding with the 14,000° C magnesium flares.

Sunrise on 6 September found two AC-47s still orbiting over Tam Ky, the third having returned to base after exhausting its ammunition. The Viet Cong who had not been killed had long since beat a hasty retreat to the nearby jungle. A message from General William C. Westmoreland, American military commander in Vietnam, praised the AC-47s for "quick reaction and professional airmanship resulting in significant loss to the enemy." While we exhausted aircrews were making our way to our quarters for some much-needed sleep, our "Gooney Birds" stood perkily on the flight line ramp, awaiting nightfall and new challenges.

The AC-47s continued their remarkable performance despite the changing strategic and tactical requirements of the war in Vietnam. In 1968 a Dragonship logged the 20,000th AC-47 combat mission while successfully defending a Civilian Irregular Defense Group (CIDG) camp in II Corps. The "Spookies" shared an almost human relationship with the ground forces for whom they provided close air support. Radio transmissions such as "We love you down here, Spooky" were not at all uncommon. This feeling was probably engendered in part by the fact that the AC-47 has been termed "one of the most effective close air support weapons in the Air Force inventory." Pragmatic considerations aside, it has been one of man's foibles to ascribe human attributes to inanimate mechanical objects. The timeless tradition of the C-47 was enhanced by the AC-47, and no one sensed this more than the pilots who flew the aircraft and the men it served and supported. The C-47 established a reputation as being the unusual airplane for the unusual job—a reputation that overshadows even its excellence as a conventional cargo aircraft. Combat operations and even routine military functions continue to generate unique and difficult challenges. The ancient C-47 has consistently fulfilled unusual requirements and performed bizarre missions for more than half of the history of flight itself, and the AC-47 marked another significant milestone in a memorable career.

It is often assumed that improved performance and greater reliability go hand in hand with advances in technology and the passage of time. Such is normally the case, and our present Air Force is an obvious manifestation of this natural progression. However, today's complicated world has produced some rather perverse problems which defy the technological progress in aviation. The Vietnam War, for example, made it painfully obvious that our high-speed, jet-age Air Force was not particularly adept at even locating elusive guerrilla bands, much less destroying them. If there is a lesson to be learned from the C-47's longevity, it might be that durability and reliability can sometimes solve operational problems more effectively than speed and sophistication.

CAPT. JAMES L. COLE, JR., is assistant professor of history at the USAF Academy. Both a pilot and a parachutist, he was an AC-47 aircraft commander in the 4th Air Commando Squadron, 1966–67.

C-54 Skymaster

JOHN F. OHLINGER

MY first encounter with the Douglas C-54 was at the Douglas Plant at Orchard Field (later O'Hare International Airport) near Chicago late in 1943. Since, as the saying goes, "everything is relative," I found myself subconsciously making numerous comparisons of the C-54 with the C-47 "Gooney Bird" on which I had amassed considerable flying time. Instead of a cramped cockpit, the C-54 cockpit seemed almost of conference-room size. One could slide into the pilot's seat without fear of getting his cranium bumped on protruding switches and other gadgetry—a noted occupational hazard for "Gooney" crews. The steerable nosewheel, a remarkable invention of those days, eliminated the vexing problems of cross-wind taxiing. Internally operated control locks did away with externally affixed battens with their attendant complexities. Four fans rounded out this delectable package—foretelling many safe and comfortable flying hours with less apprehension of the dangers of engine failure than in the case of the two-engine variety. I noted with some satisfaction that a new crew station had been added—the flight engineer—situated on a jump seat directly between pilot and copilot. For some reason, I formed the opinion that this was a definite status symbol that moved the pilot from the working class to the executive category. This opinion was reinforced later when I learned that Air Transport Command had authorized navigators, radio operators, and flight attendants as regular crew members. The "Gooney" crews of this time never had it so good.

We usually entered the C-54 through the rear cargo door, climbing either a ladder that was part of the airplane equipment or an externally provided loading ramp. There was also a small crew door just behind the crew compartment, but this was seldom used.

These were the days prior to air crew standardization and the vigorous adherence to checklists. Hence, for starting engines the crew loosely collaborated in assuring that fuel valves were open, cowl flaps open, wing flaps up, master ignition on, engines properly primed, mixture and ignition applied at the proper time as each engine was turned over by the

DOUGLAS AIRCRAFT C

C-54 Skymaster in flight.

starter. Mixture controls were located almost out of sight of the flight engineer, who eventually took to selecting the correct one by feel. Failure of an engine to start could frequently be traced to the flight engineer's having fingered the wrong control.

Although the steerable nosewheel greatly facilitated ground handling, there were other problems. Recommended rpm for taxiing was 800–1,000. However, at this low engine speed, particularly on hot days, the plugs had a tendency to foul; if they were not cleared the result could be an aborted mission. One alternative was to taxi at higher rpm—say 1,200—but this brought on another problem: at this power an excessive use of brakes was required to keep the taxi speed down to safe and manageable limits. Brakes on the early C-54s were very likely to overheat, leading to brake lockage—or at the worst, brake fire—so this alternative to the fouling problem had to be used with caution. Another option was to taxi out on only two engines, No. 2 and No. 3, and then start up 1 and 4 in the run-up position. When only two engines were used for taxi, 1,200 or 1,400 rpm could be safely used without fear of either engine fouling or brake overheating. However, this required two engine starts away from the flight line and hence without the protection of a fire guard; it was widely condemned by supervisory personnel.

Engine run-up and preflight check differed little from that of other prop-driven aircraft of the day: oil pressure, fuel pressure, hydraulic pressure, oil temperature, cylinder head temperature, mag check, etc., all within limits. One notable addition was the check of the two-stage supercharger. Just before commencing takeoff roll, the internal control lock had to be released and control surfaces checked. To preclude takeoff with the control locks engaged, Douglas had thoughtfully provided a pin suspended from the ceiling of the cockpit on a ribbon which could be reeled up when not in use. The locking mechanism was on the cockpit floor and was spring-loaded in the disengaged position. The pin was inserted in the device to hold the locks in place. Thus, when the locks were engaged, a broad red ribbon extended downward from the ceiling as warning that all was not as it should be. Despite this obvious indication there were more than a few aborted takeoffs due to locked control surfaces.

Takeoff was greatly facilitated with the use of nosewheel steering up to about 60 mph, when rudder control became effective. At 90 or so, depending upon gross weight, the aircraft eased effortlessly into the air. Climbout was accomplished at 120 mph, 35 inches of manifold pressure, and 2,350 rpm. Engine failure on takeoff, the ever-present danger in the C-47, was of little concern to C-54 drivers. Loss of either inboard engine was hardly noticeable. Control problems encountered with the failure of either outboard engine could readily be overcome with minor adjustment of trim tab, even with a full load. Maximum gross takeoff weight was 64,000 pounds; maximum gross landing weight was 56,000 pounds. For military emergency missions, gross weight as high as 72,000 pounds was authorized for takeoff.

Since the aircraft was not pressurized, normal cruising altitude was usually between 8,000 and 14,000 feet. With supplemental oxygen, cruising as high as 20,000 feet was possible through engagement of the supercharger. As to cruise power settings, the fine art of cruise control had not been perfected in the early days of C-54 operations, hence each pilot developed his own rule of thumb. Some insisted on straight 30/20 at all times—30 inches of manifold pressure and 2,000 rpm. Others insisted on constant airspeed—usually 180 mph. At high gross this required excessive power at the early stages of long-range flight with gradual power reductions as gross weight was reduced, as fuel was burned off, and airspeed tended to increase. METO power (maximum except takeoff) was 40 inches and 2,550 rpm, and there were a few intrepid and impatient aviators who took this literally and insisted on cruising just below this setting. (I am here again speaking of the time prior to standardization boards. Late in 1944 things began to improve as the idea of standardized flight procedures began to take hold.) The C-54 carburetor was the automatic type; it could be set to the auto-lean position that would automatically adjust the fuel flow to the proper fuel-air ratio depending on altitude. However, there was a manual range between auto-rich and auto-lean which some pilots used in lieu of the fixed positions. One pilot of my acquaintance claimed he could identify an improperly adjusted carburetor by the color of the metal tarnish just outside the exhaust stacks. He was an ardent advocate of manual adjustment and did his best to convert others to this theory, with little success.

Compared to other aircraft of similar size at that time, the C-54 was extremely light on the controls, very maneuverable; and this was prior to the invention of hydraulically boosted control surfaces. The airplane could be flown manually for long periods without excessive fatigue to the pilot, but it had a fairly reliable autopilot which we usually used for long-range operations.

The prime feature of the C-54 that brought out the high admiration of the flying fraternity in those days was its great range and cargo-carrying capacity. Although early versions had to rely on fuselage tanks for extended range, cutting down on cabin cubage, later versions carried all fuel in the wings—a total of 3,600 gallons. At conservative power settings, fuel consumption on a long flight could be reduced to 200 gallons per hour (50 gallons per hour per engine); an endurance of 18 hours could be expected from full tanks. As a consequence the C-54 was able to outstrip all other contenders as the vehicle for global air support for U.S. forces in World War II. A distant contender at this time was the cargo version of the Consolidated B-24 known as the C-87. As rapidly as additional C-54s came off the assembly line and crews were trained, the airplane became the workhorse of the Crescent Caravan, a military airline of the Air Transport Command operating from New Castle Army Air Base, Wilmington, Delaware. Crescent's scheduled runs eventually spread through Europe, Africa, and India as far east as Calcutta.

For instrument operations the C-54 was remarkably stable. Precision approaches using ILS or GCA (new inventions at this time and by no means universally trusted) were no problem whatever. Even in severe turbulence the aircraft seemed to have an innate affinity for the straight and level and could be brought back to an even keel quite readily despite the most severe gust. However, the airplane did have one dangerous potential known as "split flaps," which was of great concern to pilots on instrument approaches. Accepted procedure called for the lowering of quarter flaps to reduce speed prior to crossing high station (then known as high cone). In the early versions of the C-54 the left and right wing flap segments operated independently; variations in hydraulic pressure and other factors could result in asymmetrical flap configuration and even, at the worst, no flaps on one side and quarter flaps on the other side. When this condition was encountered unexpectedly—especially at night on solid instruments—the results could be disastrous. A number of fatal crashes were later attributed to this cause. A modification that interconnected the left and right flaps solved the problem once and for all.

The best landing technique in the C-54 was the power-on landing (about 15 inches manifold pressure) until touchdown. This was especially useful in gusty or crosswind conditions or at high or uncertain gross weights. (The latter was all too common an occurrence in World War II; if you knew your weight plus or minus 1,000 pounds, you were doing well.) The tricycle gear configuration permitted "grease jobs" of a quality previously unheard of. However, the airplane was not immune to the bounce; I have ridden through crow-hop landings that would do credit to the old "Goon." This usually resulted from too low airspeed, too high level-off, and excessive nose-up attitude, followed by a controlled crash. Although the airplane was most forgiving of goofs of this nature, the operation of Murphy's law was clearly evident; that is, if it's possible to do something wrong, someone will find a way to do it.

For short-field landings the technique was to bring the airplane up into an extremely nose-high attitude, full flaps and power on, holding this attitude as long as possible after touchdown. When the nosewheel touched down, flaps were raised immediately and full braking applied. Under certain loading conditions the tail skid might scrape the runway, but this caused no structural damage since the skid was equipped with a hydraulic strut to dampen the impact. It has been reported that Royal Dutch Airlines KLM made tail skid landings routinely in their short-field operations in Southeast Asia.

Although the C-54 was admirably built for operations in all climes, it exhibited some strange characteristics in extremely cold weather, like Thule Bay and Sondrestrom, Greenland. For one thing, the seals on the landing gear oleo struts would shrink, allowing leakage of hydraulic fluid from the struts, thus effectively destroying their shock-absorbing action. Taxiing on a rough surface in this condition was somewhat akin to operating an automobile with no springs. A landing perforce had to be smooth to avoid fracturing the gear. If the condition was known to the crew, due precautions could be taken on landing. Unfortunately it could and frequently did happen in flight unbeknown to the crew. On extension the landing gear would appear normal, and the crew, unwarned of the condition, would allow the oleo to immediately hit bottom on a normal landing. (It was not possible to make a visual check of the landing gear from the cockpit of the C-54; however, it could be observed through the navigator's drift meter, and this instrument was frequently pressed into service for this purpose when some doubt existed that the gear was down and locked. Some pilots distrusted the visual and audial gear warning signals—horn and lights —and made this a standard practice for all landings.)

An important item in the preflight check was to see that the struts extended the proper amount. Proper extension for the main gear was about 2¾ inches and for the nose gear, slightly more than 3 inches. These dimensions equaled roughly the height of a standard cigarette package and a king-size cigarette package, so it was not uncommon to see flight engineers using these objects as a gauge for strut extensions. Nonsmoking flight engineers could only eyeball the situation.

Another cold-weather hazard concerned the fuel tank selector valves. To change tanks, say from main to auxiliary, one simply actuated a set of switches on the control pedestal between the pilot and copilot. By a pulley and cable linkage the tank selector valves were changed, causing fuel to flow from the tank thus selected. At extremely low temperatures some part of this complex linkage could become stuck, rendering it impossible to change tanks. This was a matter of grave concern if the flight at hand depended on the use of auxiliary fuel to get to destination. Fortunately this condition was not permanent; persistent manipulation by the flight engineer could get the obstinate valves unstuck, but not without some nervousness on the part of the flight crew. Associated with the fuel tank selector switches was the cross-feed system which permitted interchange of engine operations among the various tanks. This was particularly useful in making available the fuel supply behind a failed engine to the remaining good engines. The cross-feed could also be used to transfer fuel from one tank to another, but this practice was not recommended; the need for fuel transfer practically never arose.

I never had occasion to bail out of a C-54, nor do I have any knowledge of anyone who did. However, the rear main door provided excellent egress for potential bailors, but caution would be necessary to avoid being impaled on the horizontal stabilizer. A deliberate, precipitous, headlong jump rather than a slow, lingering departure would insure against this

Interior of passenger model of C-54. Note the Mae Wests in pouches and the sleeping bags in the overhead racks.

contingency. Likewise, I am not aware of anyone having ditched a C-54, but experts generally conceded that the airplane had good ditching characteristics. It was believed that a lightly loaded airplane would probably stay afloat for some time. It was recommended that the rear cargo door not be jettisoned before ditching for fear of admitting a large amount of sea water on contact. Two over-the-wing removable panels could be used to evacuate passengers quickly. For the crew up front the sliding glass panels beside the pilot and copilot positions could be used if these persons were not unduly obese. (There was no weight-reduction program in effect in the services at this time, and consequently our outfit had a few renegade blimps who would never have made it through this exit.)

The early C-54s carried a significant amount of special equipment, but most of it was common to that being installed in production line versions of contemporary combat airplanes such as the B-17 and B-24. LORAN (long-range aid to navigation) was a new development that greatly eased the work of the bubble-chasers and bolstered the confidence of the pilots in their work. VHF radio was a fine substitute for the old "coffee grinders," but it did not immediately replace them since some ground stations were very tardy in updating their transmitters. ILS receivers (then known as SCS-51 in U.S. Army jargon) were installed in most C-54s, but this equipment likewise was not immediately useful because of the lack of ground transmitters. Radio altimeter and a crude airborne radar set for severe weather avoidance and instrument navigation rounded out the special gear on the C-54s of this period. As primitive as it may appear in this day of advanced aerospace technology, the C-54 appeared to be almost a gift from heaven to war-weary "Goon" pilots like myself.

Deicing equipment in the C-54 was similar to that in other current large aircraft. (The heated wing was still some years away.) Inflatable leading edge deicer boots, carburetor heat, and prop deicer fluid were the sum total of the airplane's equipment for combatting this formidable hazard. But the profile of the flight surfaces was such as to cause the airplane to accumulate less ice than others, and what ice was gathered could be disposed of by the boots. We dropped a number of B-17s and B-24s into the North Atlantic because of wing ice, but no C-54s disappeared for this reason, although they were operated along the same routes in the same seasons of the year.

Late in 1945 the Crescent Caravan received orders from the Pentagon to begin operation of the world's first scheduled around-the-world flight. Starting and ending point was Washington National Airport, and relief crews were posted in advance at strategic refueling points. I had the honor of piloting the initial leg of the inaugural operation from Washington to Bermuda. The passenger list included many prominent journalists of the day such as Fred Othman and Inez Robb. The flight took off on schedule amid much fanfare and publicity, and we reached Bermuda without incident. En route a fine steak dinner was whipped up by specially selected flight attendants. We changed crews at Bermuda, and I returned to Wilmington aboard another C-54. I learned later that the original airplane didn't make it all the way and another was substituted. This was unfortunate, since the initial airplane I took to Bermuda had a special paint job to suitably advertise the nature of the flight, and its interior was fitted in a decor appropriate to the status of our distinguished passenger list. (Standard models of the C-54 were not designed for passenger comfort.) Despite its problems, the flight was a historical milestone of sorts and certainly demonstrated the global airlift capabilities of the C-54 and the Air Transport Command. Although far overshadowed since by high-flying jet transports, the whole idea of a world-encircling air operation was astounding at the time. It might be noted here that the same operation—but with different airplane types—has continued without interruption to this day. It was originally called the Globemaster; later it was renamed the Diplomat and is today known as the Embassy run. From time to time it has had to bypass India due to denial of overflight rights by this nation.

Some weeks later while on leave in my home town of Toledo, Ohio, I was amazed to discover the amount of publicity that had been given the flight in the local press. Although the newspaper accounts correctly stated my rather minor role in the whole affair, I found that my adoring public generally had the misconception that I had flown the entire around-the-world operation single-handedly. Being a swinging bachelor at the time, I did little to efface this hero image except when pressed with ridiculous questions such as "How did it feel to fly across the Himalaya Mountains?" I had to admit then rather sheepishly that I had flown only from Washington to Bermuda—a mere five-hour flight.

During World War II LT. COL. JOHN F. OHLINGER was engaged primarily in air transport operations in C-47s and C-54s in all major theaters of combat. He returned to active duty briefly in 1951–52 and again in 1956. He received an appointment in the USAF two years later and retired in 1974.

The F-80 Shooting Star bagged a MIG-15 in the first jet air battle over North Korea in 1950.

Colonel Keeler named his F-80 for the Pennsylvania weekly newspaper he edited and published prior to his recall to military service.

F-80 Shooting Star

JOHN W. KEELER

WE were homeward bound to Britain at 24,000 feet, north of Würzburg, Germany. It was late 1944. Our squadron of Thunderbolts was flying cover for a box of B-24s. Somebody bellowed, "Hey, Daily Lead, we got one of them blow-jobs at two o'clock low!" As we rolled into the attack, I had my first glimpse of a jet aircraft. It was an impressive but short glimpse. At that time there were not many aircraft that could outdive the Thunderbolt, but here was one climbing faster than we were diving. Needless to say, no one got a shot at the German jet, and we would see more of them before V-E Day.

But this is not a story about the famed Messerschmitt 262, nor about the great Thunderbolt. It is a story that, for me, started that day with a burning desire to fly a jet fighter. It is a story about the first combat-tested jet aircraft in the U.S. military inventory. It is the story of the F-80 Shooting Star.

It was six years from that day north of Würzburg before I crawled into the cockpit of an F-80 for my first solo jet flight. In the intervening years I had watched the development of the jet arm of the U.S. Air Force. Lockheed seemed to have the inside track in the fighter business, and while as a "Jug" pilot I had said many uncomplimentary things about their Lightning in World War II days, I was impressed as I learned of the advances of the XP-80. The first XP-80 had flown in January of the same year that I had glimpsed that ME-262. It was 132 days from drawing board to flight; it had reached the almost unheard-of speed of 582 mph and gone to 39,000 feet. The first Army Air Force squadron was equipped with P-80s in March of 1945, and the P-80 had shattered the speed records from coast to coast and at the Cleveland National Air Races.

It was at Williams Air Force Base, Arizona, where I was to train to be a jet flight instructor, that I first came face-to-face with this beautiful and impressive bird, the F-80 Shooting Star. (We were still calling it the P-80 at that time.) The first TF-80s (T-33s) had arrived at Willy, and I had five dual rides before crawling into the cockpit. It was tight even for a 160-

pounder like me, and I remember thinking as I strapped in that it was much like a Mustang cockpit.

The plane was 34 feet 6 inches long, 11 feet 4 inches high, and had a wingspan of 38 feet 10 inches. The instrumentation was primitive compared to today's fighter cockpits, but it was a great improvement over our World War II birds. "Toggle switches, circuit breakers, and clocks" was my first impression as I sat there getting familiar with my surroundings. The airspeed read in miles per hour and fuel consumption in gallons per hour. As I was taking in the mass of gauges and switches, I remembered and smiled at a comment I'd heard many years before. My father had owned a Ford car in the 1930s, and a droll friend had asked as he looked over the dash, "George, did you get blueprints with this?"

There was one incongruous item in the cockpit of all the F-80s at Williams. Some months before, a pilot had crash-landed and then burned because he couldn't open the jammed cockpit canopy. Now at Willy each F-80 had a sawed-off baseball bat strapped forward of the left console—a primitive but effective tool to use to batter one's way out of a locked cockpit.

For one raised in the prop fighter era, one of the most startling revelations on that first jet flight was the slow response when the throttle was advanced for takeoff. Anyone who had flown the Thunderbolt or Mustang remembered the immediate surge down the runway when that 12-foot prop grabbed the air and how the bird leaped off after a few hundred feet of roll.

Not so in that pre-afterburner era of jet fighters. On a summer afternoon in that Arizona desert there was always some last-second "puckering" before the bird staggered into the air off the end of Willy's 6,300 feet of runway. Takeoff roll was seldom computed, and a wet finger held in the breeze usually decided go or no-go. On a cross-country flight to Denver some weeks later this was nearly my undoing. The mile-high city on a hot day is never a setting for a short-field takeoff, and I blew dust and sagebrush for what seemed to be halfway to the Kansas state line before getting airborne from Lowry Field. Heavy emphasis was later placed on computing takeoff rolls.

A simultaneous revelation on takeoff for a former propeller driver was the astonishing absence of torque. For one whose right leg was longer than his left from years of holding 2,000 hp straight down a runway, the phenomenon of getting airborne without manhandling the rudder control—indeed with little or no rudder pressure—was nearing the miraculous.

Like all airplanes the F-80 became a beautiful machine with gear and flaps up, airspeed increasing, and climbing skyward. But there was an added beauty for the F-80—its ease of handling. For anyone who had wrestled World War II fighters into steep turns at 400 mph, the fingertip control of the roll axis of the F-80 was also a miracle of the age. In retrospect, after flying Century Series and other high-performance fighters, the F-80 still stands out as the easiest-to-fly aircraft I ever operated. Its hydraulic-boosted aileron control gave a new dimension to fighter performance and fighter tactics.

It was a light airplane, relatively speaking: clean, with internal fuel only, the F-80B weighed 12,744 pounds; with tip tanks full of JP-1 it grossed out at 15,215 pounds. Its J33 engine gobbled up 120 gallons climbing to 30,000 feet and covered 120 miles of ground getting up there. A calibrated airspeed of 260 mph would true out at about 410 mph at this altitude. The flight operating charts said you had enough fuel to escort bombers (and that's what the F-80 was designed for) 530 miles, drop the

tanks, fight for 15 minutes at 100% rpm, and turn around and get home with 50 gallons in the traffic pattern—enough for one go-around if you didn't get lined up the first time.

In the pattern the 80 was stable and honest. The 360° overhead approach for jet fighters was out of vogue for a period of time, and the landing pattern in the early operating instructions was rectangular.

Even the published tech orders on the F-80 took on a jet-age appearance. They were the first I had seen with true readability and with any humor. Straightforward instructions such as this appeared in boldfaced type: "WARNING: Do not spin this airplane with drop tanks installed. Jettison tanks if accidental spin develops." And even if redundant, this double emphasis was impressive: "This airplane is controllable up to a Mach number of .8. This limitation must be observed." There was also a loose permissiveness in the flight instructions that doesn't appear in today's manuals: "In general, acrobatics should not be attempted below 10,000 feet until the pilot becomes familiar with the speed at which the airplane can gain and lose altitude."

Cockpit of the F-80.

Every prop driver who has transitioned to jets has had that sinking sensation on his first formation join-up when he has chopped the throttle and continued to streak on past his exasperated leader. The clean aerodynamics of the F-80 took some getting used to, and even the speed brake didn't come close to giving the braking power one had with four 12-foot blades out front. But the 80 was a jewel to fly in formation once it was mastered. It was a stable aircraft, and even with the underslung drop tanks it took a minimum of effort and jockeying of the throttle to hold fingertip alignment.

On several occasions at Williams I flew with the Aerojets, one of the first jet demonstration teams in the world. The F-80 was superb in this role. With no drop tanks, wings could be tucked in to a four-foot overlap on the lead; the formation performed more as a single airplane than any demo team before or since.

It was early 1952 before I got my orders to the 8th Fighter Bomber Wing, then flying out of K-13 near Suwon. The three squadrons were flying F-80Cs, the latest model of the Shooting Star. If I had been impressed with the F-80 as a jet trainer, my respect for it was increased tenfold in its role as a combat aircraft. As a gun platform and weapons delivery system I found it to be par excellence in the Korean War. Even with an outmoded sight the F-80 was superb at putting bombs on the target and in its close-support role. Designed as a high-altitude air-to-air fighter, the Shooting Star wound up in Korea as a fighter-bomber. Lockheed engineers must have cringed at the loads of bombs, rockets, and napalm that we hung on the wings of this little bird!

While it was no match for the performance of the swept-wing MIG-15 that we sometimes faced in the North Korean skies, as a ground attack machine it was unsurpassed. The six .50 calibers in the nose gave a good concentration for strafing trains and vehicles as well as hosing enemy bunkers and gun positions. The guns were also fine protection for low-level attacks with napalm.

But it was as a bomber that the F-80 excelled, carrying a thousand-pounder tucked under each wing. We initiated dive-bomb runs in echelon from 11,000 to 13,000 feet. A steep run—60–70°—was best for accuracy. The book said to release at 3,500 feet to bottom-out of the dive between 2,500 and 2,000 feet. When it was necessary, the book was forgotten; with an F-80 one could bore into 1,500 feet, release, and still get away without picking up bomb fragments from the plane ahead. Dive-brakes were used in this form of delivery, and speed seldom exceeded 350 mph at bomb release.

Skip bombing in the F-80 was effective against the railroad tunnels in the mountains of North Korea. On one particular mission against a supply train that had taken refuge in a tunnel, I simultaneously released two delayed-fuse thousand-pounders into the tunnel entrance, banked over the tunneled mountain, and saw bomb blast come from both ends of the tunnel. The remainder of the four-ship flight sealed the train in the mountain. A good afternoon's work in any war!

Encountering MIGs in the 80 was not dreaded by U.S. pilots. Quite to the contrary, we welcomed the few tangles we had with them. It was an F-80 that knocked down a MIG-15 in the first all-jet air-to-air battle. The superior speed and zoom capability of the MIG gave it an immediate advantage, but if its pilot made the mistake of slowing to the 80's speed for a fight, the MIG was outturned and outgunned by the straight-winged Shooting Star.

All jet aircraft are supersensitive to battle damage, and the F-80 was no exception. But its simplicity and lack of complicated control and fuel systems gave it a special toughness and battleworthiness. On at least one occasion over Korea a battle-damaged 80 flamed out as it was limping home. Unable to get an airstart the pilot glided southward. His innovative flight leader dropped to the rear, gently nudged the nose of his 80 into the tail-pipe of his flamed-out wingman, and "pushed" the crippled bird back over friendly territory. That's togetherness at its best.

The greatest satisfaction for a fighter-bomber pilot in Korea came in the form of a good mission in direct, close support of our ground troops. About 60 percent of our F-80 combat missions were close-support type. I have cherished for more than 20 years a letter from Major General J. C. Fry, then commander of the Second Infantry Division in Korea, which addressed the close-support role of the F-80. The letter came to the 8th Fighter-Bomber Wing the day after a particularly hard-fought ground and air battle for an infamous piece of front-line real estate known as "Old Baldy." The letter is indeed a tribute to the men and to the F-80 Shooting Stars they flew:

> I wish to express on behalf of my command our heart-felt appreciation for the superb combat assistance given us on 5 November. I personally observed the low level attacks made which, without question, hurt the Chinese tremendously. In fact, one ground observer reports seeing a Chinese .50 caliber gun receive a direct hit by napalm. My considered opinion is that the air strikes were extremely effective.
>
> A by-product of the air attack was the tremendous lift it gave the Infantry. I was on "Old Baldy" when some of the attacks were made, and without exception, officers and men alike were pleased and happy over what they saw. I am sure the pilots concerned would have been immensely proud if they could have heard the men say, "It takes real guts to go in and do that job."

The last F-80 came off the Lockheed production line in June 1950. In six and a half years 1,732 Shooting Stars were manufactured. The U.S. Air Force, U.S. Navy, and five South American nations used the airplane as a first-line fighter at some period of time until December 1972. My last flight in an 80 was in 1959, when I ferried one to the Colombian Air Force.

The T-33, the most famous jet trainer in the world, is the dual-control, tandem-seat version of the F-80. In the decade of the '50s, 90 percent of the Free World pilots trained in this aircraft. This "big brother" of the F-80 has been the standard jet trainer in 40 foreign air forces.

On a recent visit to the Air Force Museum in Ohio, as I stood before the polished Shooting Star on display there, I recalled a story concerning the first test flight of the F-80. As Lockheed designer "Kelly" Johnson approached the plane with test pilot Milo Burcham he said, "She's all yours, Milo. Treat her nice. Find out if she's a lady or a witch."

For one who trained, taught, and fought in the 80 she's a lady—a revered and respected lady.

COL. JOHN W. KEELER is director of information for USAF in Europe with headquarters in Ramstein, Germany. In World War II he served with the 8th Air Force in England, flying P-47s. Recalled to active duty during the Korean War, he flew 166 missions in the F-80.

F-84 Thunderjet

CHARLES D. BRIGHT

FOR the pilot who was new to the straight-wing F-84 Thunderjet its appearance on the ground was no preparation for the labors of takeoff. Even with centerline tip tanks, which it carried for normal flights, it appeared to be sleek and speedy. Without any external fixtures it looked even racier with its small stubby wings. Takeoff would prove to be contrary to expectations, a fitting introduction to an airplane with unusual qualities. This was especially true for pilots who made the transition to the 84 from a piston fighter.

In contrast to the F-51's spirited takeoff—which gave a sense of impending flight shortly after the roll began—the F-84, though it was powerful, gained speed slowly and felt heavy even at liftoff. It did this under the best of conditions, using almost two miles of runway—a marked contrast to the F-51's half-mile.

Under the worst conditions, with full fuel and armament loads on a hot Korean summer day, the takeoff had no margin for safety. In this case the pilot was forewarned. Auxiliary fuel, bombs or napalm, and sometimes rockets or jet-assisted takeoff (JATO) bottles crowded onto the narrow undersurfaces of the F-84 gave it an overloaded appearance. The pilot could say to himself, "Well, the kitchen sink isn't there, but only because there is no place to hang it." Fully loaded, the gross weight of the E model was 10 tons.

The pilot used as much runway as possible, running up to full throttle with the brakes locked. This gave him 4,900 pounds of thrust. At the beginning of the roll, when there was little lift, the weight would cause the struts to hit bottom often. As the speed slowly built up, a careful reference was made between the airspeed indicator and points chosen by the pilot to mark progress down the runway so as to measure performance by "feel." (This was before "tech orders" enabled a pilot to calculate progress speeds and check them against markers placed at the runway sides.) The progress was more critical than it would be today, for the Air Force did not use barriers (arresting cables for jet fighters) for many years

REPUBLIC AVIATION

F-84 Thunderjets in flight.

of the F-84's service life. An estimate by the pilot that flying speed would not be attained meant releasing the externally mounted armament and fuel tanks and then trying to brake to a stop on the graded dirt overrun or, if desperate, to retract the landing gear and slide to a stop on the plane's belly. The F-84 had a robust landing gear, and more than one survived undamaged in the overrun or beyond where most other fighters would have come to grief with collapsed gear.

If all appeared to be going well, the externally mounted JATO bottles were fired. Later, and more accurately, these were called RATO, for rocket instead of jet. Although welcome, the added thrust from these engines always felt disappointingly small at a time when the pilot knew all the runway had to be used at best. The F-84 used two or four of these engines, each producing 1,000 pounds of thrust for 14 seconds. But RATO

was not all blessing. While the first pilots to take off had a clear view ahead, those following had to contend with a thick white smoke over the runway from earlier RATO firings. They not only had to strive for best takeoff performance but also had to include reference to the instruments for blind flying. Although smokeless RATO was later developed, newer fighters have a much better system for thrust augmentation in their afterburners.

When flying speed was reached, the 84 pilot did not fly his plane off the runway. Instead he mechanically placed the joystick in the full back position against the seat, making sure that no stray object, oxygen tube, or radio wires impeded complete travel. The F-84's nose would rise and the plane would unstick at about 160 mph when fully loaded. After a few moments, at slightly increased speed to make sure that the aircraft would not settle back to the runway in its near-stall state, the gear handle was moved up. As speed built up, the flaps could be "milked up" (brought up in steps). Over a designated area the rocket engines could be dropped. As drag reduced, there was a marked, rapid increase in speed. The nose could be lowered rapidly, and, no longer sluggish, the 84 moved forward in swift, pleasing flight.

The Thunderjet carried eight high-velocity five-inch serial rockets and six .50-caliber machine guns with 1,800 rounds of ammunition. After rockets were fired, the launching devices could be retracted to provide a streamlined wing surface.

The Thunderjet now presented a contrast to its behavior during takeoff. The basic airplane had low drag; even with its centerline tip fuel tanks, an F-84 kept at full throttle and low altitude would soon be pressing on its Mach limitation (Mach .82, which is about 620 mph at sea level on a standard day). Acceleration when not burdened with the drag of any external stores was both exhilarating and frustrating. The straight wing and conventional tail were relics of the piston era and imposed such low limits on performances as to make the F-84 a most unusual aircraft. Instead of almost always flying comfortably below its structural limits as do most aircraft, the 84 had the power and streamlining to reach those limits quickly. It was frustrating to have the power to go faster but be forced to observe the airframe limits.

Inattention to or deliberate violation of the F-84's speed limitations below 15,000 feet resulted in a pitch-up—a sudden, uncontrollable nose-up attitude—and the airframe normally could not withstand the radically changed airflow. The result was disintegration, with the wings failing. At high altitude the plane could be forced through this limit and still be controlled, but this resulted in a rough ride, for the airflow around the F-84 above Mach .82 was not smooth. The effect was like that of clear air turbulence. The battering on the airframe at 40 (indicated) mph past the Mach limit was so heavy as to raise fears of structural failure, even though the 84 was built in the Republic tradition of rugged airplanes.

Just as the pilot could drive through the limits above 15,000 feet, he could, with diligence, stay within the limits below it. By planning entry speed, with careful throttle handling and monitoring of the airspeed indicator, he could split-S into a vertical diving attack from 10,000 feet above the ground. The result was excellent ordnance accuracy together with low vulnerability to flak.

Pilots were generally most unhappy with the need for frequent attention to structural limits while in combat, the more so because the limits condemned the F-84 to inferiority in combat against the MIG-15—a more modern design. The 84 did not even have the usual shelter of the slower fighter—a smaller radius of turn. It simply could not turn with agility. Using both hands the pilot could force a hard turn at high speed. That is, he could enter it, for although he could achieve three Gs momentarily, the airspeed indicator would rapidly unwind. The result was a failure to turn effectively and a sacrifice of available speed.

The straight-winged F-84s, outclassed in air-to-air combat in Korea, are credited with eight MIG-15s destroyed in combat against a loss of eighteen. One F-84 pilot with credit for two MIGs on one sortie was asked how he did it. He answered something like this:

> Well, the first flew in front of me and I squeezed the trigger! I got him. Later two got on my tail and I couldn't shake them. I thought, "They'll never follow me through a pitch-up, and maybe the wings will stay on." So I dove and rammed the throttle full forward. As I approached the Mach, I tried to help the plane into pitch-up early in hopes of easing the load on the wings. The wings stayed on! And sure enough, the MIG's couldn't turn that corner! One didn't pull out of his dive and he's my second victory.

The 84 in this double victory was inspected and found to be sound. But where it had been one of the nimblest planes in the wing, it became both lame and a hangar queen—a real "dog."

Air Force pilots never forgave the F-84 for its inferiority to the MIG-15. Thus, although the 84 did the same yeoman fighter-bomber service in Korea that Republic airplanes have done in all three of our modern wars, it never approached the popularity with pilots of the P-47 and the F-105, both of which had air superiority capabilities. This was unfortunate, for its qualities made it a superb fighter-bomber. The high speed increased the effective range of the F-84's ordnance and permitted operation at the extreme limits or outside the effective range of enemy flak. Its speed meant that the front lines could be reached quickly—in around 20 minutes from a ground-alert scramble. On none of my missions nor any I heard of did the 84s arrive too late to help the ground forces. There was fuel for loiter of around 30 minutes, and I never had to cut short a sortie because of lack of fuel. The F-84's sturdiness allowed it to operate under rough airfield conditions and to take battle damage. The lack of maneuverability produced a solid, steady gun platform. This was enhanced by an adjustable power boost system for the ailerons, with which one could select the ideal boost setting for his conditions of flight. There was no torque or need for rudder control. The gunsight computed for bombs and rockets as well as for the

Cockpit of F-84.

six .50-caliber machine guns; we could easily line up and smoothly track a target from two miles out, and the results could be impressive.

General Otto P. Weyland, Commander of the Far East Air Forces, said that the F-84 attacks on the Toksan and Chasan reservoirs in 1953 were "perhaps the most spectacular of the war." F-84s flew 86,408 sorties and dropped more bombs and napalm (55,987 tons) than any other Air Force fighter in the war; they fired only a small share of the rockets, however. Only 153 F-84s were lost to enemy action, and only 98 of their pilots were killed.

The qualities that produced a great gun platform made the F-84 a fine plane for instrument flying. It was smooth and easy to control at any instrument flying speed, so blind flying was easier than in many other planes. The same properties made it an easy plane to land. One type of pattern was circular out of a pitch (a turn with 90° of bank). Speed brakes were extended and throttle brought back to almost idle. Wingmen pitched later for spacing and delayed dropping gear and flaps to avoid the need for power in the pattern. When the airspeed fell into the region where the gear could be extended without damage, it was dropped and the flap handle put down. The flaps would extend themselves gradually as the airspeed slowed to the 160 mph used for a normal final approach (40 mph faster than the F-51s). If the pilot set up the appropriate glide to the runway, he would be nose low. Shortly before contact with the runway he could bring back the stick. The nose would respond and the plane would take up a landing attitude. But the flight path would not noticeably alter; there was no flare or float at normal airspeeds. Touchdown would be easy but noticeably one with finality out of the mushing descent. Crosswind or gusty landings were no problem—in sharp contrast to an F-51, which was sensitive and had to be handled with care through the whole landing sequence and landing roll. If a go-around was necessary, engine response time was comparable to that of the F-51: the 84 had slower engine acceleration, while the F-51's throttle shouldn't be rammed forward at low speeds because of the high torque.

The F-84's qualities enabled it to be in the vanguard for several modern fighter activities. It pioneered in the use of both flying boom and probe-and-drogue aerial refueling for Air Force fighters. Using aerial refueling the F-84s made notable ocean crossings en masse as early as 1952. The F-84 was the first single-seat fighter capable of delivering a nuclear weapon. Its stability and ease of maintenance contributed to its choice as the aircraft for the first Thunderbird demonstration team, formed in 1953.

For all the honors, a pilot will also appreciate the airplane that brings him home. I once had engine failure while 25 miles from base at 8,000 feet and 300 mph. After the automatic turn towards home and climb to the best glide speed, the distance was unchanged, but there was now 11,000 feet of clearance above runway elevation. Since the F-84 had a glide ratio of 14 miles forward progress for the sacrifice of one mile of altitude, it appeared feasible to try a dead-stick landing. (Had bailout been necessary, most F-84s had an explosive-driven ejection seat. The canopy was explosively released, before the seat was fired, by raising the hand grip on the right armrest. Then the pilot positioned himself, raised the left grip, and squeezed the grip's trigger. After ejection he would kick clear of the seat. If the pilot chose or was in a nonejection seat model, bailout was similar to that in piston fighters.) The choice on this flight was to take the plane home, yet it seemed unbelievable that the ground-loving F-84 would actually float all that distance when the glide of a powerless F-51 was like the legendary "streamlined brick." Course was set directly for a base leg, where the landing gear was pumped down by hand. The approach proved to be ideal with a deliberate slight overshoot. The dead-stick landing turned out to be a "piece of cake."

Watching the miles slip quietly and effortlessly by while the altimeter unwound with a casual slowness in engineless flight, it was hard to believe I was in the same ground-loving beast that had to be pried into the air for takeoff. But this was only one of the contradictions and surprises of an airplane with many unique and unusual properties. Nearly 4,500 were built, and they were used by a large share of the Free World's air forces. Obscured by the great F-86, the Republic F-84 nevertheless figured large in the shaping of the jet age. General Weyland called it the workhorse of the Korean War. It deserves an important rank among America's combat aircraft.

LT. COL. CHARLES D. BRIGHT was a B-17 lead navigator in the strategic air offensive against Germany and an F-84 pilot in the Korean War. He is retired from the USAF.

The F-86D with radar in the nose. Designed for high-altitude interceptor missions, the Sabre has proved excellent for close formation flying.

F-86 Sabre

CECIL G. FOSTER

I HAD recently been recalled to active duty and was reporting to Nellis Air Force Base in Nevada when I first glimpsed the F-86 Sabre. It appeared to maneuver like a bumblebee in flight, although I later found that it carried a lot more sting. I was originally assigned to train in the F-80 but was later selected to upgrade in the F-86. This was one of the highlights of my career. I still recall how we F-80 pilots would gaze hungrily at the Sabre as we rode along the flight line to our Shooting Stars.

On the day that the new assignments were made public, we immediately ran to look the Sabre over. To enter the cockpit it was necessary to place the hands and feet in the kicksteps and climb, as on a ladder. The cockpit seemed filled with an enormous amount of equipment. It was a small cockpit with a sliding, motor-driven bubble canopy. The instrument panel had the standard instruments plus an improved airspeed/Mach indicator, altimeter, fuel flow indicator in pounds per hour, and rate-of-climb indicator. The throttle quadrant was located on the left subpanel and incorporated an air start button, a speed brake switch controlled by the thumb, and a microphone button for transmitting on the UHF radio. The stick had a form-fitted hand control with a trigger switch, trim control, nose-gear steering button, and bomb release (pickle) button.

As the pilot looked out of the cockpit, the swept-back wings gave him the feeling of riding well forward on a speeding dart. Visibility throughout the horizontal plane was outstanding. The pilot sat high in the bubble; the only blind spot was underneath the body, wings, and empennage. It appeared to be almost impossible for an enemy to sneak into firing position at the F-86 when there was an alert pilot at the controls.

Early model Sabres had wing slats on the leading edges for improving aerodynamic capabilities at slow speeds; these were manually locked in place after the craft became airborne and unlocked prior to landing. On later models the wing slats moved back and forth automatically, depending on the existing aerodynamic conditions. This caused some difficulties when operating at extremely high altitudes or when flying near the maximum performance levels; however, they provided added lift automatically at high G

NORTH AMERICAN AVIATION

The F-86F in flight.

loading and/or low airspeeds. Later models (F-86F) and modified early models had a slightly longer wing without the wing slats. This modification provided added performance at extremely high altitudes with a decrease in turn capability in the lower altitudes.

Six .50-caliber machine guns, located three on each side of the nose, provided awesome power. They were synchronized to a point approximately 1,000 feet in front of the aircraft, but their effective range exceeded 2,000 feet, and on a few occasions enemy aircraft were shot down at ranges exceeding 3,000 feet. These successes were undoubtedly attributable to the assistance provided by the computing radar gunsight. The ammunition was linked and the mix consisted of armor-piercing incendiary, tracer, and high explosive.

Starting the engine was a simple and rapid operation. As an example, one day in 1952 as I was passing through the squadron operations area at K-13, Korea, I was unexpectedly called to assume alert duties. Moments after selection, I was told to scramble—before changing into flight gear! While getting strapped into the cockpit, I was assisted by a fellow pilot who climbed astraddle the nose of the fighter facing rearwards, reached into the cockpit, started the engine, and then jumped off to the side. I became airborne in less than three minutes from notification. No warm-up was necessary for the aircraft or its component systems—a tremendous asset to a forward-based fighter. Taxiing this aircraft was simple; nosewheel steering used the utility hydraulic system and was instantly available by activating a button on the stick grip. In the rare event of a utility hydraulic system failure, the aircraft could be steered by the use of wheel brakes.

Most missions were initiated with a formation takeoff, usually in elements of two. The control surfaces were hydraulically operated, giving the F-86 instant response to control inputs, and throttle response was outstanding. A perfect wing position takeoff was quite easily flown and was a very enjoyable experience. The lead aircraft would signal engine run-up for his element by rotating a raised finger, then signal for a simultaneous brake release by a head nod, followed by a smooth throttle advance to about 98%. This permitted the wingman sufficient leeway in power to maintain good wing position throughout the takeoff. As airspeed increased, a slight back pressure on the stick lifted the weight off the nosewheel and permitted an extremely smooth takeoff.

Instant and postive control was always available from takeoff through landing. The F-86 was the only aircraft I have flown that gave the pilot confidence that he could do any maneuver he desired, at any time, with full assurance of safety throughout. For example, while flying at cruise power settings, the pilot might want to perform a loop; he need only pull back on the stick, push forward on the throttle, and casually complete the maneuver. Although the airframe had G limitations, it could sustain more than the pilot—even when he was augmented with a G suit.

Fuel for the F-86 had a kerosene base with a maximum internal load of 3,000 pounds. Fuel consumption at 45,000 feet was 1,200 pounds per hour (the same as idle on the ground). The effective range was increased considerably with the use of two drop tanks. Normally, taking off from K-13, Suwon, Korea, a climb to and cruise at 38,000–40,000 feet to the Yalu River would consume all of the fuel from the drop tanks. These tanks were retained unless enemy aircraft were engaged, in which case they were jettisoned by simply pushing a button (commonly referred to as the panic button).

Once free from the tanks, the F-86 maneuvered magnificently. Our Fighter Wing instructions were to leave the Yalu River area with no less than 1,000 pounds of fuel, since the distance to K-13 was 250–300 miles. Once we were chasing a MIG-15 at 1,000 feet near the Yalu River when the wingman called, "Bingo fuel" (meaning 1,000 pounds of fuel remaining). Disengaging the enemy, we climbed at Mach .93 to 45,000 feet, cruised to within 100 miles of K-13, then pulled the throttle to idle and left it there until after landing. We still had 250 pounds of fuel remaining! For comparison purposes, modern jet fighter aircraft are in an "emergency fuel" state even in the traffic pattern with only 1,000 pounds of fuel remaining. Top speed for the F-86 was Mach .97–.98; however, normal cross-country cruise varied from .86 to .93.

Landing techniques were similar to conventional fighter aircraft: enter initial (350 KIAS [knots indicated airspeed] would do quite well) and when reaching the near end of the runway, enter an 80–90° bank while simultaneously extending the speed brakes and reducing the throttle to idle. The bank was maintained, and when the proper speed was reached, the gears and flaps were extended and checked. The 360° idle-power pattern was usually very comfortable and easy to complete for the flight leader; however, strong wind conditions or wingman position required an adjustment in technique. Throttle response, if power was needed, was readily available.

Later techniques were developed that required establishing a downwind leg prior to entering base leg. This was necessitated by wind miscalculations or weak pilot techniques that resulted in aircraft mishaps; the change provided additional time and a chance to adjust the pattern to fit the conditions. The F-86 had a good glide ratio (although not as great as the straight-winged jets) which provided a nice flare prior to touchdown on the two main gears. The nose lowered gently to the runway as the airspeed decreased. Positive control was available throughout the landing roll. Wheel brakes were very efficient and greatly reduced the landing roll but were seldom needed on a 6,000-foot runway.

Training for combat in the Sabre consisted of ten sorties at Nellis Air Force Base; these included a solo checkout, aerobatics, engineering, formation, high and medium altitude air-to-air gunnery, and air-to-ground gunnery missions. It was possible in the early models to pull too many Gs in the gunnery patterns, resulting in a violent high-speed snap roll frequently followed by a spin or spiral. Later models were improved with the automatic wing slat action, eliminating this undesirable trait.

The F-86 became an extension of the individual at the controls. It could be as docile, smooth, beautiful, vicious, deadly, speedy, daring, or safe as the pilot desired. The redundant systems throughout the aircraft provided safety margins which encouraged the pilot to go anywhere, anytime, against all odds, for he was confident that he had the best and safest fighter ever built. I never sustained damage from either enemy aircraft or antiaircraft gunfire throughout my Korean tour of 100 missions, including approximately 35 dogfights.

Combat maneuvering was superb. The Sabre excelled or equaled the MIG-15 in all aspects except for service ceiling. The MIG-15 could climb higher and in some cases faster than the Sabre, but it was no match for the F-86 below 40,000 feet. In one dogfight beginning at 38,000 feet, my wingman and I attacked a group of 24 MIG-15s flying in three flights of eight. The resultant action lasted over 45 minutes and produced one MIG-15 destroyed and one damaged. Many other battles involving similar odds were experienced, and in each instance the F-86 proved to be a superior aircraft.

Defensive/offensive tactics were universally referred to as "fluid four" maneuvers. A thorough description of these tactics would require more space than available here: briefly the basic unit is an element of two aircraft flying approximately line abreast. Each of these is augmented with a wingman, greatly enhancing the defensive capability. Several flights of four can be used in a single formation, but the most effective use is achieved by retaining the flexibility of flights of four. The distance between aircraft within a flight expands as the altitude increases, thus compensating for the change in radius of turn at higher altitudes.

When used in a ground-support role, the Sabre compared favorably

SAC MUSEUM

A "MIG killer" home to roost after its last flight.

in payload with the F-80, while retaining its excellent defensive capability after releasing the payload.

Ejection was a simple action—pull up the armrest (which jettisoned the canopy and locked the shoulder straps) and squeeze the trigger in the armrest. I had supreme confidence in the system and cannot recall a single instance when it failed.

One idiosyncrasy of the F-86 was the necessity of physically entering the nosewheel well to reset the emergency hydraulic system after it was activated from the cockpit. It was common practice for the crew chief to use this system to open the gear doors for maintenance on the aircraft, but if the system was not manually reset it was impossible to raise the landing gear after takeoff. This occasionally occurred when actions were rushed prior to a combat mission, resulting in the annoyance and embarrassment of an aborted sortie.

There should be no doubt in the reader's mind that I thoroughly enjoyed every minute in the F-86. Although by today's standards the Sabre was small and slow with minimal firepower, there never was an airplane so beautiful, dependable, maneuverable, and deadly when in the right hands. What more can I say about the airplane that made me the top living jet ace at the time of my rotation from combat?

LT. COL. CECIL G. FOSTER flew the F-86E in the Korean War, the F-86D and F-101B in the all-weather interceptor career field, and the F-4D over Vietnam as commander of a tactical fighter squadron.

NORTHROP CORP.

The F-89D Scorpion in flight over Long Beach Harbor in Southern California in 1952. Wingtip pods carried 2.75-inch rockets and Falcon missiles. Electronic aiming and automatic triggering equipment enabled the pilot to direct his fire with pinpoint accuracy in all types of weather.

F-89 Scorpion

WAYNE C. GATLIN

THE best way I can describe seven years of flying the F-89 Scorpion would be to say that what she lacked in beauty, she more than made up for in reliability and mission capability.

My first airborne encounter with the F-89 came in May 1955 at the dedication of the Richard I. Bong Memorial at Poplar, Wisconsin. Our part of the flyby was to form the horizontal portion of a cross in four F-94Bs, while the vertical portion of the cross was formed by five USAF F-89Ds. This cross was led over the memorial site by a civilian P-38. I remember my amazement while flying line-abreast off the huge rocket pod-tip tank of an F-89; the air was a bit rough, and the sight of that big black tank bouncing up and down was mighty impressive.

The first production model was flown in 1950. The early models were equipped with six 20 mm cannon, and pilots who flew them then were able to rack up some very fine air-to-air gunnery scores. The F-89 saw many weapons configurations until it arrived as a J model. Gone were the cannon, replaced by a 250-gallon nose tank, and rockets in the tips were replaced by 600-gallon fuel tanks. The F-89H was the first fighter to see armed service with the Falcon missile, and the F-89J (our model) had the distinction of being the first U.S. fighter to carry air-to-air nuclear armament. It was first to fire the weapon in operation "Plumb Bomb" at the Proving Ground, Yucca Flats, Nevada. We had the F-89 over seven years, finally ferrying part of our fleet to the storage depot at Tucson and the rest to the Aberdeen Proving Grounds, Maryland, where they were to become cannon fodder for weapons evaluations.

The F-89J carried 2,365 gallons of fuel (15,372.5 pounds), which gave it tremendous range. During exercises we were able to go far north into Canada on Combat Air Patrol and remain on station for extended periods of time. This gave the SAGE (Semi-Automatic Ground Environment) staff a great advantage in air battle planning and execution. Prior to the F-89 we were able to do all of our weapons training right at home station; we had an air-to-air range out over Lake Superior that had been completely adequate for the .50-caliber guns of the F-51 Mustang and the F-94B Starfire and the 2.57 folding fin aerial rockets of the F-94C. The F-89J with its nuclear-tipped missile "Genie" required a much larger range, and we had to deploy to Tyndall Air Force Base, Florida, to fire the training version of the "Genie." My reaction the first time I fired the weapon was that it sounded like a freight train roaring by, and I was surprised at the intense contrail that it left. Tactics dictated an immediate breakaway, but most pilots were prone to hold off for a few seconds to watch the con and the spotting charge burst out near the target.

With a wing span of 59 feet 8 inches, length of 53 feet 10 inches, and height of 17 feet 6 inches, the F-89 covered quite a bit of ramp. It grossed out at almost 45,000 pounds. Power was provided by two Allison J35s rated at 7,400 pounds of thrust each with afterburner. When you initiated the F-89 afterburner there was no big kick in the seat of the pants as with most afterburners; they sort of went "poof," and you could sense slight acceleration. One radar observer described it as "sort of like a barge leaving the dock" when the afterburners were lit.

The F-89 needed no ladder to the cockpits, which were a long way off the ground; kick steps and handgrips were provided to mount the steed. The only trick was to remember to start the climb with the right foot; otherwise you wound up several feet in the air dangling your left foot in space, unable to step onto the wing because your right foot was your only means of support. The first time I climbed into the cockpit, I was delighted with the roominess—not since the P-47 "Jug" had I seen that much elbow room. The fuel control panel quickly drew my attention, for it looked extremely complicated with a myriad of lights and switches; it turned out to be a pretty simple system to operate, with the capability to balance fuel, to cross-feed to one engine, and to dump the fuel from the tip tanks.

Scorpion displays a Falcon guided missile in firing position.

The F-89 in flight.

Of all the jets I've flown, the F-89 had the simplest starting system. We started the left engine first by just hitting the starter switch momentarily, checked for a rise in oil pressure, and then moved the throttle to "idle" when the engine reached 7.5% rpm. The starter disconnected at about 26% rpm, and the engine stabilized at about 50% rpm. Right-engine start was the same as for the left.

Directional control during taxiing was maintained with a steerable nosewheel. Pre-takeoff check consisted of placing throttles full open and checking exhaust gas temperatures and rpm. We then lifted the left afterburner finger switch and checked for thrust surge; next the right afterburner; then the check for fuel siphoning, the brake release, and the start of the takeoff roll. Directional control was maintained with the steerable nosewheel until the rudder became effective at about 70 knots indicated airspeed (IAS). We kept the nosewheel on the ground until we reached our predetermined nosewheel liftoff speed (120–138 knots IAS, depending on gross weight); then we eased back on the stick, allowing the aircraft to fly off the ground at its applicable airspeed 124–143 knots IAS).

Gear up when definitely airborne, flaps up at 160 knots IAS minimum, and gear and doors indicating up and locked. We then accelerated to best climb speed. For a max power (afterburner) climb we started out at Mach .69 at sea level, gradually increasing Mach to .79 at best cruise altitude—normally 30,000 feet. We usually climbed out at military power (100% rpm and non-afterburner) to conserve fuel, starting out at Mach .48 (315 knots IAS at sea level) and increasing to Mach .66 at 30,000 feet. Takeoff in the F-89 was not one of its finer points. The takeoff roll in summer got especially long, and with a high field elevation such as at Denver, Colorado, you had a real thrill in store. A zero wind takeoff from Denver on a 70° day took a good 9,000 feet of runway. The aircraft would barely stagger into the air, the ground seemed to refuse to release the airplane.

The climb to cruise was long and tortuous—almost 30 minutes to 30,000 feet—and once we reached cruise altitude we had to "hump out" or never make our destination. This consisted of climbing a few hundred feet above level-out altitude, keeping power up, and then diving down to altitude, keeping military power until we got indicated cruise airspeed. Then and only then could we reduce power for normal cruise, which was about 90% rpm. A good rule of thumb for cruising the F-89 was 4,000 pounds of fuel per hour to get a 400-knot true airspeed. This was 2,000 pounds per hour per engine, and we would only have to add or subtract the winds-aloft effect to get our ground speed. We used 1,000 nautical miles as a good round number for a no-wind, no-alternate-required, cross-country planning factor.

Once airborne, the F-89 proved to be a fine aircraft to fly. One of my first desires was to see how that much mass would handle aerobatically. Much to my delight it was smooth and fully aerobatic, though a bit heavy on the over-the-top maneuvers. In the traffic pattern it could really bend around with those big wings, and the actual landing was a "piece of cake." All flight controls were 100 percent hydraulically actuated. A sideslip stability augmentor provided good dampening of the high-speed Dutch roll, assisted in making coordinated turns, and helped provide a stable firing platform.

The stall in the airplane was a mild pitch-down, with drop-off usually to the left. Recovery from stalls was made by lowering the nose slightly and adding power. Intentional spins were prohibited; however, the airplane would not spin inadvertently and had no dangerous spin characteristics. Conventional spin recovery techniques were effective.

One of the finest features of the airplane was the split-aileron speed brakes. We could make letdowns up to 30,000 feet per minute without exceeding 350 knots IAS. The brakes were especially effective for controlling airspeed and altitude during approaches and reduced ground roll appreciably when moved to full open *after* touchdown.

We normally flew a standard 360° overhead pattern. Entry to initial approach was at 275 knots and 85% rpm. At the break we opened the speed brakes and decelerated to 195 knots, closed the speed brakes, put gear down and flaps to takeoff position, and turned onto final approach at 170 knots. Full flaps on final, maintaining 85% rpm until landing was assured. Speed brakes had to be used with caution on final to prevent too rapid deceleration and stalling out. Final approach was 132–157 knots IAS depending on gross weight. Throttle to idle when landing was assured, and speed brakes open after touchdown. Main wheels touched at about 116 knots, and nosewheel down before reaching 111 knots. It was a very nice aircraft to land.

We all swore that Northrop must have subcontracted for the F-89 wheels to a farm implement manufacturer, for they looked as though they had just come off a tractor on the north forty. The tires were imbedded with short steel wires that gave the aircraft very good traction on snow and ice. The gear doors were strong and durable—some said they came off the side of a battleship. I know of two instances where the aircraft touched down on the runway with one main gear retracted but the gear door open, and the aircraft was undamaged except for the grinding off of some of the metal on the gear door; in both instances, the door alone had supported the weight of the aircraft.

We lost one F-89 in seven and a half years of flying in one of the most severe weather areas in the United States. The lone accident was caused by fire in both engines, and the pilot (alone on the flight) ejected successfully, although he suffered hand burns from having to reach for the ejection handles with fire coming through the cockpit floor by the handles.

I purposely haven't said much about the fire-control system for lack of space; however, the F-89 with a good aircrew team of pilot and radar observer was a match for any target that could be put up against it. The fact that it had no infrared heat-seeking weapons reduced its capability against low-altitude targets, and its overall lack of a high-speed dash capability hurt if the target ever got past the F-89. But more often than not the old bird got everything head on and was perhaps the best all-weather interceptor we had at the time. The twin-engine concept more than paid for itself over the years, for we had a number of aircraft return on one engine. In mid-January 300 miles north of Duluth, Minnesota, one appreciated that capability.

In our eagerness to get operationally ready in the F-89, we jumped at every chance to get a sortie that filled one of the requirements. It so happened that my first night intercept mission was between layers of clouds on a black, moonless night. The intercept phase went fine, but the eventual formation join-up and penetration were hairy; the aircraft's external lighting was not conducive to formation flying, and the vertigo I suffered during the ensuing recovery was monumental!

My first hassle with the F-102 proved to be delightful, for the Deuce jockey fought my kind of dogfight and elected to turn (and the Deuce will turn, as I learned in over four years of flying it after the F-89). I got on his tail without effort and stayed there with ease. Of course he could have left me at any time had he plugged in his burner, but apparently he was low on fuel and just sort of slunk away with his tail hook behind him.

Yes, what the Scorpion lacked in beauty, she more than made up for in reliability. Like the B-36 she never fired a shot in anger, but she took part in the defense of the United States and more than adequately provided her share of deterrence against any possible aggressor.

COL. WAYNE C. GATLIN, a World War II veteran, is commander of the 148th Fighter Group, Minnesota Air National Guard, stationed in Duluth. He has logged nearly 6,000 flying hours, mostly in fighters.

A camouflaged F-105 en route to a target in Vietnam in 1966.

F-105 Thunderchief

JERRY NOEL HOBLIT

THE target was in the vicinity of Thai Ngyen. Leo Thorsness was leading the Iron Hand Flight; Tom and I were flying No. 3. Our plan was to split the elements about 50 miles out from the target: Leo would cover north of the target and Tom and I would take the area to the south. But the flight plan fell out as soon as we entered the package, since the weather was very poor. Leo didn't call for the element split, and I assumed that he wanted to keep the flight together until we either weather aborted or found suitable weather right next to the target. Very suddenly we broke out of the cloud-covered hills and I saw the missile.

The missile was tracking Leo, and it was obvious from his transmissions that he was well aware of it. He was in a hard left turn going over some very small hills. The missile was in a hard right turn. From the geometry of it, it looked as if the missile had been fired at a nearly tail-on aspect to the flight. We were very low. Leo hugged the ground and the missile scraped off on one of the hills. I looked in the direction the missile had come from just in time to see a large splash in the klong, probably the booster, and just past that point I saw something I never expected to see: the side view of a camouflaged missile site. I was looking under the netting and could clearly make out the launchers, although it seems hard to believe since my range had to be 4–8 miles. The next action was obvious and automatic. I advanced the throttle and brought in the afterburner, forgetting about Leo. I kept my eyes on the site, because I knew that as I gained altitude I'd lose it if I didn't keep the position firmly fixed.

I had six CBU-24s, and the sight was set for a manual 45° 5,500-foot AGL (above ground level) delivery. In combat you never hit your conditions exactly and normally make aim point corrections to compensate for dive angle or airspeed variations, but I was so preoccupied with keeping the target in sight that I just put the pipper (gunsight) on the center of the site and reacted when it looked about right. As soon as I felt the ordnance leave, I started a jinking pull-out; when the time came for bomb impact, I rolled up to take a look. I never had such a lucky hit in my life. The pattern covered the site exactly, and immediately two missiles blew up on the launchers; there's no mistaking the characteristic orange smoke when an SA-2 explodes. I didn't see where the wingman's bombs hit. He had six Mark-82s, and he said at the debriefing that he saw his bombs go off on the site also. That was the first missile site "kill" we had made. It came in March 1967 on my sixty-ninth mission—my thirty-fourth as a Wild Weasel.

In 1960 the F-105 had not yet received its final epithet of "Thud"; it had various—mostly unkind—nicknames such as "Squat Bomber" or "Hyper Hog." The majority of fighter pilots believed the bar story that Pentagon bomber generals had selected the Air Force's next fighter over the objections of the one or two resident Air Staff fighter pilots, disregarding a host of better aircraft in the process.

My first impression led me to believe these stories. The airplane was on the Nellis ramp—out of commission—after an eventful flight from Seymour-Johnson, where the Fourth Wing had the first F-105Bs. It was huge. My education up to that point, at the hands of former F-86 pilots, had led me to believe that the F-100 was a big airplane. The F-105 was much larger—more than 60 feet long and weighing more than 36,000 pounds without external fuel or stores. Contributing greatly to the aircraft's impression of size was the extreme length of its main gear, caused by the midwing configuration and the necessity to have tail clearance on take-off rotation.

Jim Sears and I approached the aircraft with the proper awe expected of young Nellis studs (a term referring to our student rather than bachelor status) who were first laying eyes on the "Air Force's Future Tactical Fighter." I tried to chin myself up on the intake to see what that looked like and found myself unable to reach it even with a running leap. Jim, although shorter, was more athletic and did manage the feat; I made a mental note that preflight checking of intakes for possible FOD (foreign object damage)—standard on every jet—was going to force me to get into shape. We were impressed by other unusual external features as well as by the size of the craft. The rakish intakes appeared very radical. The aircraft had a bomb bay designed for a nuclear weapon; a large piston driven by an aircharge ejected the bomb from the aircraft. The speed brakes consisted of four petals aft of the vertical stabilizer that completely surrounded the fuselage. Few airplanes up to then had incorporated spoilers for roll control. The canopy looked strange, and the port for the M-61 Gatling gun had an ominous and effective air about it.

Later I learned that the intake design was used to incorporate a movable plug which changed the intake's geometry (automatically) above Mach 1.4 so that intake shock waves were properly positioned up to Mach 2.0. Checking the intakes was not a preflight item; the external preflight consisted of little more than a general viewing of the aircraft from four sides. During most of the Thud's productive lifetime the bomb bay was filled with a 390-gallon fuel tank, and the bomb bay turned out to be an unnecessary design that detracted from the aircraft even in its nuclear mission. The speed brakes were very effective and caused no pitch or yaw transits at any speed, including Mach 2. There was, however, something inherently spooky about an airplane that automatically opened the speed brakes a few degrees to allow the afterburner to light. The spoilers contributed greatly to the honesty of the aircraft's control, particularly at slow speeds. I often wondered if the F-100's adverse yaw characteristics could not have been improved with spoilers instead of the more conventional

REPUBLIC AVIATION

A fully loaded F-105 taking off.

ailerons. The canopy was of double design that circulated air between the layers to prevent fogging. The M-61 was, and remains, an effective air-to-air or air-to-ground weapon, not only on the F-105 but on the A-7 and the F-4E as well.

After that first view of the F-105B in 1960, I went to Germany to fly F-100s with the 49th Tactical Fighter Wing; in the fall of 1961 I returned to Nellis to check out in the F-105D. That began my gradual conversion to "Thud driver" both in spirit and in fact. The airplane had been optimized for low-level penetration and delivery of nuclear weapons, and the D model was equipped to accomplish this mission in all weather conditions. The airframe, armament, and electronic equipment also permitted the F-105D to perform day-fighter, limited-interceptor, close-support, and conventional interdiction missions.

At Nellis we learned to fly the aircraft and all the basics of the aircraft's systems, and on returning to Germany we completed weapons qualification and became alert-qualified in the aircraft. To become fully combat ready required that we learn new techniques of radar navigation and bombing, and in the European F-105 wings a great deal of emphasis was correctly placed on this aspect of flying the Thud.

While still at Nellis I noted the first indications that pilot acceptance of the F-105 was growing. Former F-104 pilots were heard to say an occasional kind word about the aircraft. No one could fail to be impressed by the aircraft's stability and control characteristics, low-altitude performance, or systems integration and cockpit layout. The D model had much more sophisticated electronic systems than the B and was easier to maintain—although still ahead of it were numerous groundings and non-pilot-related accidents.

Despite the airplane's size, the impression from the cockpit was fighterlike. The cockpit was of average size, and visibility except to the rear was good. In its day the F-105 was the most complex single-place airplane ever built, and even today few aircraft can match the Thud's range of capabilities. Yet its cockpit was very logical, easy to learn, and easy to manage.

Airframe-related systems were simple, and most of the cockpit was devoted to weapons systems and navigation equipment.

To accomplish the aircraft's primary design mission, four essential pieces of gear were integrated and displayed to the pilot: a ground-mapping and terrain-avoiding radar, a doppler and navigation computer, an autopilot, and a bombing computer. The pilot's displays were arranged in a T in front of him, along with integrated tape and gyro instruments just above the radar scope. The ground-mapping radar was used in conjunction with the doppler and navigation computer to navigate to and identify a target. The radar scope used a 90° sector scan with variable ranges from 13 to 80 miles. It was the designer's intention that the majority of flight time would be spent with the scope in a contour-mapping or terrain-avoidance mode, allowing the pilot to maintain the closest possible profile to the ground. Ground mapping was to be used selectively for navigation point and target identification. In practice we found that the allotted flying time allowed us to be barely proficient in radar navigation using only the ground mapping and usually flying our legs on MEAs (minimum en route altitude). The autopilot was designed to be used in at least a stick-steering mode from takeoff to landing and was essential for the low-level, all-weather mission. In Southeast Asia an attempt was made to used the F-105 as a night or adverse weather, low-level bomber—without outstanding success. My experience with the F-105, A-7, and A-6 leads me to believe that radar, low-level, conventional bombing is generally unproductive and a waste of time in a single-place aircraft. It is a very viable tactic, however, for nuclear ordnance.

The Thud, along with several other aircraft, employed the integrated tape instrument display. The instrument cross-check was so easy with this display that new Thud pilots would frequently perform better after one flight than they had after many in their old airplanes.

The toss-bombing computer (TBC) was an analog device tied into the other aircraft systems and was meant to be used for both conventional and nuclear delivery. We seldom used the TBC for conventional bombing but relied on the manually depressed sight instead. In retrospect, I believe that we erred in this and should have spent more pilot and maintenance time on this system and used it as the primary bombing system in Vietnam.

Engine and aircraft flight systems were not complex. The J-75 engine was started either by pyrotechnic cartridge or external air source. Once rpm was developed, the pilot brought the throttle to idle and starting fuel was auomatically sequenced. Idle rpm was 68–71%. An air turbine motor (ATM), driven by compressor air, supplied power for both the AC generator and the utility hydraulic systems. This ATM was located forward and to the right of the cockpit and was very noisy, especially on the ground. Once started, with the ATM and AC generator on the line, all subsequent checks were straightforward and could be accomplished in less than five minutes in coordination with a crew chief, by hand signals or through ground interphone. I have been wheels in the well (gear up) in four minutes in an alert aircraft—starting from the Officers' Club!

The F-105 carried large amounts of varied armament and was capable of being refueled either by probe and drogue or by boom. Engine-driven pumps provided power to the dual hydraulic flight controls. A ram air turbine was available for emergency electric and flight control hydraulic power. Unfortunately a hit that caused loss of one flight control hydraulic system usually got them both. I later came to appreciate the manual backup system in the A-4 and consider it essential that flight control hydraulic lines be physically separated and that fly-by-wire systems be thoroughly investigated.

Although the F-105 was optimized as a fighter-bomber, it had day-fighter and limited-interceptor capabilities. At one time it had the best MIG-killing record in Southeast Asia. Its antiaircraft armament consisted of an interceptor-type radar display, lead computing sight, M-61 gun, and Sidewinder missiles. In terms of performance it was usually outclassed by the F-80, F-4, MIG-19, and MIG-21 but generally superior to the F-100 and MIG-17. It could beat the MK-6 (Canadian Sabre), F-86, and MIG-15, providing the Thud driver did not try to slow down and turn with his adversary and generally kept his head above his emotions. In the Southeast Asia campaign over North Vietnam the Thud's day in the sun arrived, and it was the mainstay of Rolling Thunder operations until the 1968 bombing halt. Two-seat F-105Fs were equipped for a surface-to-air missile hunter-killer mission. These Wild Weasel aircraft have added an interesting new dimension to aerial warfare.

The F-105 was an easy aircraft to fly as long as you did it fast. It was built to operate at low level and very high speed. This it did exceedingly well. It did not do well at altitude (in terms of performance, stability and control were excellent in all flight regimes) and demanded high speed in the traffic pattern. Takeoffs were frequently above 200 knots. Landing approaches, although flown with an angle of attack instrument, were sometimes in the 200-knot range also. Nevertheless, its good brakes, drag chute, and power response were such that such speeds were no particular problem. I can remember few takeoff rolls over 6,000 feet. A no-drag-chute landing seldom ended in a barrier engagement.

In the air the aircraft simply had no peculiarities. A spin or out-of-control situation, such as an adverse yaw induced out-of-control maneuver, was almost nonexistent. It took extreme, usually intentional, mishandling to get the bird to spin. Few pilots succeeded, and fewer still were fast enough to beat the airplane in doing its own spin recovery. The only control anomaly was a tendency for a nose-down pitch change when the gear was retracted forward into the swept wings.

When the airplane was new it could achieve Mach 2 easily. As the airplane grew in service, however, the expected thrust uprating of the engine did not materialize. The craft did grow in weight and drag because of various modifications, so both its top speed and range were substantially reduced. Above Mach 1.4 it was slowed with speed brakes instead of with a throttle reduction. In 1961 a man chasing me on a Mach 2 run had to put out his speed brakes to stay behind my slower aircraft. By 1967 few F-105s could achieve Mach 2 on a test flight.

There is no question in my mind that the F-105 and her pilots and EWOs (Electronic Warfare Officers) wrote a page in the history of aerial warfare in Vietnam. Whether they did so because they were inherently great or just happened to be there when it all happened is a judgment I cannot make. This, however, I know: it was an honest aircraft—one that reflected care in design and engineering, and it was a credit to all who conceived and built it. It educated us and remains the standard according to which I judge other airplanes. I prefer the A-4's size and economy, the A-7's digital integration and accuracy, and the F-4's excess power for a fight; but if I had to choose one airplane today to go to war tomorrow, it would have to be my Thud.

In 1961–67 LT. COL. JERRY NOEL HOBLIT flew the F-105 at USAF bases in Germany, Japan, Thailand, and the United States. His subsequent duty has been with the Air Force Test Pilot School, the Navy Air Test and Evaluation Squadron, and the Office of the Deputy Chief of Staff for Research and Development at Headquarters, USAF.

F-106 Delta Dart

JACK GAMBLE
PATRICK K. GAMBLE

TO put it simply, the F-106 Delta Dart is a honey. And I emphasize the "is" because after fifteen years in my inventory it is still a fine fighter and a joy to fly. My first association came in 1960 when I was given the opportunity to command an F-106 squadron. My first impression, formed on my first day in the squadron, is the same impression that still comes to me every time I cross the ramp to the "six" I am scheduled to fly.

When you see a "six" sitting on the flight line, you have to be impressed by its sleek beauty. It is the kind of aircraft that seems to be flying even when waiting silently on the ramp. The clean, slim, Coke-bottle fuselage is enhanced by the elegant delta wing and sturdy rakish vertical fin. These features all combine to produce a feeling in the viewer that this machine was meant to fly.

From a distance her sleekness masks her size; only when you are standing by the wing do you realize that this baby is as long as a C-47 and can gross over 40,000 pounds. But the power of her Pratt & Whitney J-75 engine augmented by an afterburner can lift her mass into the air and up to 40,000 feet and more in minutes.

The F-106 was designed as an interceptor, and the air-to-air role has been her mission ever since. Not once has she been called on to sling bombs or rockets from her wings. Instead her punch is safely stored in a missile bay and exposed only at the moment of launch. Originally she was designed to stand ready against the threat of invading bombers. Today that role has been expanded to include air-to-air combat against other fighters. Her inherent good design, improved by air-to-air refueling and the capability to carry the 20 mm Gatling gun, make her a worthy air-to-air opponent even now in her venerable years.

When the F-106 came into the inventory it boasted several innovations. Although it bore a family resemblance to the F-102, it was a new aircraft with more sophisticated systems. The area rule fuselage and vertical tape flight instruments were two of the more noticeable. The MA-1 weapon control system is the electronic heart of the airplane, providing digital computer displays to the pilot which solve the intercept or navigation problem related to the tactical mission. Part of this system is contained in the tactical situation display—a rather large circular map located forward of the control stick between the pilot's knees; by using various TACAN station selections, it shows in map form the area surrounding the station. An interceptor bug on the face of the display continuously locates the aircraft visually in relation to its position over the ground. A target bug is also available to assist in displaying the intercept problem to the pilot in the tactical mode or for other functions in the navigational mode. Other features include automatic control of the aircraft via ground-air data link, automatic navigation, and coupled ILS approach. Many other sophisticated features make it a complex aircraft; the pilot must have a thorough knowledge of all of its systems if he is to stay abreast of all the information available to him and fly the airplane to the extent of its capability.

Cockpit entry is conventional, making use of a special ladder which hooks over the cockpit rail. The clamshell, clear-vision canopy is well out of the way in its full open position. The pilot places his back-type parachute in the cockpit first and connects it to the seat survival kit. Next he connects the parachute firing lanyard to its receptacle on the ejection seat, completing an essential step in the sequenced, one-motion ejection system. Once he stows his other gear it is an easy step over the rail, making sure as his feet ease down into the rudder alleys that a careless toe does not come into contact with the secondary canopy jettison lever located on the lower left forward part of the seat. Out of respect for this particular lever, a "six" pilot never puts anything in his lower left flying suit pocket and always keeps the zipper zipped.

After donning the chute and fastening seat belt and shoulder harness, the pilot has completed the links that provide a rapid and effective ejection system. The one-motion system is started with the pilot raising either hand grip. The canopy leaves the aircraft, and seat ejection follows. Seat-man separation occurs, then forced parachute deployment and survival kit deployment. The system is designed to work from zero feet–zero speed up to 450 knots. Certain combinations of critical attitudes and sink rates introduce limitations, but generally the system is highly effective.

Getting ready to start the engine involves a complete cockpit check to make sure that every switch and lever is properly positioned and every instrument is properly set or giving the right indication. Prior to cockpit entry, the pilot and his crew chief have already completed a walk-around inspection of the aircraft to insure that pressure gauges and fluid levels are in order, leaks have not developed, ground safety pins are pulled, and the aircraft by tacit agreement between the two is ready to fly. When the cockpit check is complete and the pilot is ready to go, he watches for the crew chief to signal that the aircraft is clear and he then is ready for the start.

By depressing the start button on the throttle and manipulating the throttle, the combustion starter is activated, with engine light off taking place a few seconds later. The start is normally assisted by an air cart and electrical power cart, although the airplane can start on its own stored high-pressure air and the aircraft battery. Once the start is complete, aircraft power is turned on and another cockpit check brings all systems on the line. Instruments such as the altimeter and engine pressure ratio gauge are set, and you are ready to taxi.

Up to this point you have been busy making sure that everything has been done properly. As you taxi you have a second to appreciate the power you hold in your left hand and the responsiveness of this beautiful machine, even on the ground. Nosewheel steering is available at the touch of a button on the stick. After engagement, control of the nosewheel is obtained by pressure on the left or right rudder pedal. Once rolling, the "six" is inclined to keep going as if anxious to get airborne; as with a spirited horse that needs a tight rein, you have to hold it in check by gentle use of the brakes.

Additional checks completed while taxiing include such things as the radar and the ground-air data link. Final checks before lining up for takeoff include canopy locked, pressurization on, fuel switches on, ejection seat safety pin out, and no warning light on in the cockpit. With clearance from the tower and the airplane lined up on the runway, the throttle is advanced all the way. The primary gauge at this moment is the engine pressure ratio gauge, which indicates whether engine thrust on the ground is suitable for takeoff. One final check that all systems are go, and brakes are released. Immediately the 16,000 pounds of thrust push you back in the seat as the "six" accelerates down the runway. A quick look at the instrument panel tells you all is O.K., and the throttle is moved outboard to light the afterburner. The bang as the burner lights and another push in the back tell you that the additional 8,000 pounds of thrust have taken hold and you are being propelled down the runway at an ever-increasing pace. Nosewheel liftoff speed of about 130 knots is soon reached, and back pressure on the stick smoothly lifts the nose to takeoff attitude. Proper angles of attack are important at this point; either too high or too low will increase the ground roll. Putting the nose on the horizon or 10° up on the attitude indicator allows the aircraft to fly at the best ground roll for the field elevation and surface temperature. Once safely airborne the landing gear must be retracted immediately since the gear-down speed can be exceeded very easily.

The airplane flies in a most conventional fashion despite its delta wing and lack of conventional empennage. It is completely responsive to the controls, and a light touch with the stick is the name of the game. Inattention or ham-handedness can result in being a thousand feet higher than you want or over on your back. When flown within its envelope the "six" has no bad habits. However, like most high-performance aircraft, if you venture outside the envelope, you do so at your own risk. The Mach 2 speed capabilities of the aircraft give it a wide range of options in its combat role, and it is a potent adversary against targets well above 50,000 feet.

With its two 360-gallon external supersonic fuel tanks, the F-106 has a most comfortable range and endurance compared with other fighters of its vintage. When afterburner is used, fuel consumption goes up and range and endurance correspondingly decrease. But all things being equal, it is no problem for the "six" to leave a West Coast base and cross the continent with only one refueling stop. If air refueling is used in a deployment, spanning an ocean becomes quite practical.

Landing an aircraft has always been the most challenging phase of flight to me, and landing the F-106 is no exception. The handling characteristics of this aircraft at pattern speeds and altitudes are excellent. The landing approach can be made from a visual overhead pattern or by use of ground controlled approach (GCA) or instrument landing system (ILS) approach. The landing gear is lowered at 250 knots and checked down by three green lights indicating each wheel. Flaps do not come into play (the "six" is not so equipped), but speed brakes are opened as the descent is started on final if under GCA or ILS. Approach speed varies with the gross weight of the aircraft as affected by remaining fuel and armament on board. Using 180 knots as a good average approach speed, altitude is held at 1,500 feet AGL (above ground level) as you approach the GCA glide path. As speed bleeds off, the delta wing configuration causes the angle of attack to increase continually. Since this subtle change is not particularly discernible unless you watch the attitude indicator and altimeter, it is easy to lose altitude gradually because outside references incline you to undercompensate for the amount of nose-up required to maintain level flight. When the glide slope is reached and the controller tells you to begin your descent, you open the speed brakes, reduce power, and establish your rate of descent. Airspeed to the knot is displayed on the vertical tape airspeed indicator, which can be cross-checked against the angle of attack tape readout. Airspeed and rate of descent are essentially controlled by power adjustments.

Approaching the end of the runway at 180 knots is a thrill to say the least, and at that speed the margin for error is minimal. Back pressure on the stick is applied and power smoothly reduced as the touchdown is approached. The main gear tires gently kiss the runway as the power hits idle. The drag chute handle is pulled, and a few seconds later a definite tug is felt and deceleration increases. At 90–100 knots the nosewheel is lowered gently to the runway by easing the back pressure on the stick, and the rollout is under way. Nosewheel steering is engaged, and gentle braking slows the aircraft down for the turnoff at the runway end. Dropping the drag chute, cleaning up the cockpit, and a careful taxi back to the ramp completes the mission. At this point any F-106 pilot has a deep sense of satisfaction.

I have flown about 400 hours in this airplane, and if I had to pick a favorite among all the fighters I have flown, the "six" would be it. It is a complex and challenging airplane to fly, but it is honest. I have enjoyed and appreciated each moment I have flown it and look forward to many more hours of association with this fine aircraft.

MAJ. GEN. JACK GAMBLE, commander of the 25th North American Air Defense Command (NORAD) Region, flies with the 318th Fighter Interceptor Squadron at McCord Air Force Base, Washington, as a combat-ready pilot in the F-106.

ON Armed Forces Day in 1961 I stood beside the runway mobile unit and watched a "fourship" of F-106s prepare to take off for their flyby. The noise was deafening, and sooty black smoke billowed out behind the aircraft as the pilots ran the engines up. I could see the element leads clearly as they nodded their heads to signal brake release, and then as the afterburners lit on those big J-75s I knew I wanted to be an Air Force fighter pilot. More than that, I wanted someday to fly that very airplane—the F-106. It was quite a few years from that day as a high school sophomore until November 1970 at Tyndall Air Force Base, Florida, when I was once again listening to an F-106 engine run up. But this time I was in the airplane and preparing to fly it for the first time. Now, three years later, I still get the same thrill listening to that engine and flying what I consider to be one of the finest true fighter aircraft in the world.

The technology behind the F-106 was pushing the state of the art in the mid-fifties, and the aircraft was the first Mach 2 production fighter. Its computerized fire control system was a revolution in avionics. Designed as an interceptor against large bomber-type targets, its speed, maneuverability, armament, and the later addition of external fuel tanks for long range were the fulfillment of the very same requirements that a successful interceptor needs today. Despite the seventeen years since the first models rolled off the assembly lines, the F-106 remains our first line of defense against an aircraft threat to the North American continent.

Many modifications have enhanced the airplane's capabilities. Originally conceived as a point-defense aircraft that would operate out of only one base for its entire life span, the "six" has been retrofitted with such items as an air refueling system, solid-state avionics components, and a clear-topped canopy (the old canopy had an eight-inch-wide steel bar running longitudinally through the apex) and soon will be modified for quick installation of the M-61 Gatling gun and a fantastic new gunsight. The designed 3,000-hour lifespan of the airframe has been more than doubled through a structural integrity evaluation. If future modification proposals are approved, the airplane will virtually have a new lease on life. It currently carries a worldwide deployment capability.

Approaching an F-106 on the ground you can't help but admire the natural beauty of the airframe. The long needle nose is angled slightly downward since the airplane sits a little "downhill." It's not a small airplane (combat weight is 42,000 pounds), and the single cockpit sits high off the ground. But the 70-foot fuselage is gracefully curved by the Coke-bottle waist or "area rule" design—one of the key reasons the airplane is able to go Mach 2. Like its predecessor the F-102, the "six" has delta wings with elevons. These control surfaces replace the aileron/horizontal stabilizer package and are on the trailing edge of the wing acting as elevators and ailerons simultaneously. Lack of flaps or boundary-layer devices dictates a higher final approach airspeed than most fighter aircraft, normally in the 180-knot range. The Delta Dart is powered by the J-75 axial flow engine with an afterburner thrust rated at 24,500 pounds and a military thrust of 16,100 pounds. One of the finest features of the F-106 is this outstanding Pratt & Whitney engine. Being a single-engine fighter, the reliability of that engine is most important, especially on missions several hundred miles out over water or up into the Canadian wilderness. Even with occasional problems of a serious nature, the engine continues to get the pilot home. I once had a main bearing failure 200 miles from the nearest suitable landing field. Despite severe vibrations and noise so loud I couldn't hear my UHF radio turned full up, I flew the 200 miles and landed safely. Upon landing I also had a primary hydraulic failure which was attributed to the hydraulic reservoir cracking from the severity of the engine vibrations. The ruggedness in this incredibly reliable engine is added insurance appreciated by the pilots.

The pilot preflight is really simple for so complex an aircraft. During the walk-around the pilot or crew chief pulls the gear pins and the safety pins for the external tanks and the tail hook. The pilot checks the engine access panels to make sure they are closed and examines fittings and lines for general condition and leaks. Certain hydraulic reservoir and accumulator gauges as well as the missile bay and the system air pressure are given cursory examination, but these are quick looks and not time-consuming. Although the pilot's checklist itemizes the preflight sequence, each pilot develops a habitual pattern that includes items not listed in the checklist. This results in the pilot preflight becoming a *very personal* action.

Climbing into the cockpit you are aware of the comfortable surroundings and ample leg room. The radarscope sits directly in front of your face. The right and left consoles are crowded with switches and dials, but the cockpit layout is convenient. When strapped in you are snug but not crowded. Engine start requires pressing the ignition button atop the throttle and listening for the familiar pop of the combustion starter; then into idle at 10% and disconnect the ground power. Once the generators are switched on the line and the radar is turned on, you are ready to taxi. There is very little to turn on after engine start in an F-106, and this makes a scramble easy. I have seen a flight of two break ground 2 minutes and 43 seconds after a no-notice active air scramble. Nosewheel steering is activated by a button on the stick, and the airplane taxis easily. ADC (Air Defense Command) squadrons perform "last-chance" just prior to takeoff. This last-minute once-over by a ground crew has spotted many aircraft malfunctions that have manifested themselves between the parking area and the runway—mainly in the area of leaks or unsecured panels that would probably come off in flight. I have personally seen a pair of chocks in the gear doors, a small nosewheel-well fire, cut tires, and large air system leaks caught in last-chance. A thumbs-down by the last-chance crew is a mandatory no-go; the pilot must go back to the parking area for a fix or, if that's not possible, a ground abort. In three plus years of flying the F-106 I have been turned back three times; twice I had to abort the mission. It goes without saying that if the additional quality control provided by last-chance has saved even one aircraft, it has been worth the time and effort.

On engine run-up you check the hydraulic pressures, oil pressure, exhaust gas temperature, fuel flow, and EPR (a measure of engine efficiency dependent on temperature). You also set the attitude indicator to show 5° nose low, and as you rotate for takeoff you raise the nose to indicate 10° nose high. This compensates for gyro acceleration error in the indicator and prevents overrotation. The pilots soon develop outside references for takeoff, such as the "put-the-pitot-boom-on-the-horizon" method. Of course these vary according to the individual's height. The same explanation can be made for landing attitudes. (Check the skid plate under the tail of

Cockpit of the F-106.

almost any F-106 and you will see the system isn't foolproof!) One last flight control check and then you release brakes. After insuring that you are rolling straight, you pull firmly on the throttle outboard of the full forward position to light the afterburner (AB). With pressure applied the throttle clicks out to the AB range. It can then be smoothly moved back and forth from min to max AB just as if you were moving it normally; AB is *not* forward of the military position but alongside of it. Full mil is as far forward as full AB, and min AB is about equal to the 92% (normal thrust) position.

There is a very definite kick in the pants, especially noticeable in the winter or in an airplane without the two 360-gallon external tanks, when that AB cuts in. Airspeed increases rapidly to the rotation speed of 120–135 KIAS (knots indicated airspeed). At this speed you pull back smoothly on the stick until the nose is raised 15°. Holding this altitude the airplane becomes airborne at about 184 KIAS. The F-106B, the tandem two-seater, flies at slightly higher airspeeds. Takeoff distance is normally between 3,000 and 4,000 feet, depending on temperature and winds. At 250 KIAS the afterburner is terminated and the airplane is accelerated to 400 knots and climbs at this airspeed until Mach .93. This Mach is held for all further climbs and cruising. If the mission is to be a practice intercept sortie, the armament safety check is completed and the IR (infrared) system is initially tuned. The IR seeker head is recessed in the top of the aircraft nose and is raised at the flick of a switch. This system allows the pilot to acquire a target by homing on the radiation of its engine exhaust and is a great aid when the radar is malfunctioning or during an attempt to track a heavy ECM (electronic countermeasure) emitter.

Soon after takeoff the pilot selects the data link receiver to begin receiving the coded UHF messages that inform the aircraft computer what type of intercept and target information is available. This information is displayed to the pilot on his instruments; the mission is not dependent on voice communications with GCI (ground control indicator) controller.

Once the target appears on the radarscope as a small blip, the pilot must use the left half of the Y-shaped stick and lock onto the target by moving the stick to superimpose a "gate" on the radarscope over the target. Once this is done, the fire control system automatically displays steering information and overtake rate.

The pilot has a choice of weapons—two radar-guided AIM-4F Superfalcons, two AIM-4GIR Superfalcons, or the AIR-2A Genie nuclear-capable rocket (sometimes called the blivet or the bean). This mixed load makes the F-106 a multishot weapon and adds versatility to combat not only against high-speed, high-altitude targets but also against high-speed, low-altitude targets. With the addition of the M-61 20 mm gun, the F-106 will have the close-in kill capability it currently lacks. All weapons are carried internally and cause no performance restrictions.

The average training mission flown by squadron pilots consists of a profile of intercepts and tactics. A formation takeoff and cruise to the intercept area is followed by low-altitude intercepts against a T-33. The venerable T-bird is equipped with chaff and an ECM pod. By varying his use of these countermeasures and varying his heading and airspeed, the target pilot attempts to cause the interceptor to miss its attack. If it is missed because of a mistake made by the interceptor pilot, it is called a "PE" or pilot error. If the attack is successful, the pilot calls "MA"—mission accomplished. Following several low-altitude passes the fighters move to the medium-altitude area where they may "bump heads" or take turns being targets themselves while the other fighters attack. A few high-altitude snap-ups complete the profile. Here the F-106 target is cruised subsonic or supersonic at 49,000 feet while the attackers combat from 34,000. The attacker must lock on, accelerate, and pull sharply up (snap-up) to fire against the high-altitude target. The maneuver is actually a simulation of the type of attack necessary to combat a bomber target in excess of 55,000 feet. Following completion of the intercepts the fighters reach "bingo fuel." This means they have to return to base because they have only a predetermined amount of fuel remaining. The formations rejoin and recover to single-ship or formation landings.

Since 1968 ADC has been training its pilots in air combat tactics (ACT). The Command-initiated idea was soon adopted by the Navy and Marines, and more recently TAC (Tactical Air Command) established a squadron of T-38s used as "aggressors" against the TAC fighter squadrons.

F-106 Delta Dart in flight.

Under the supervision and direction of the Interceptor Weapons School (IWS) at Tyndall Air Force Base, Florida, ADC conducts College Dart. This ACT program features the F-106 flying against F-4s, F-8s, and A-4s from Navy, Marine, and TAC squadrons. Pilots get a full week of advanced air-to-air training against an aircraft very different from their own. College Dart has demonstrated the fantastic air-to-air potential of the F-106. Only within the last four years has this most underrated fighter been given some of the recognition it is due. Closely approximating the MIG-21 in overall performance, the F-106 is (in 1974), in the opinion of most fighter pilots who have flown in it or against it, the best production air-to-air machine in the U.S. inventory. Its acceleration enables it to engage and disengage comfortably. The ability of the delta wing to turn at high altitude is used to great advantage. Because it is a single-seat aircraft, ADC has developed the "Six Pac" tactics group to enable the F-106 pilot to best employ the aircraft in a fighter-versus-fighter environment. The tactics are based on an element of two aircraft both employed as shooters but maintaining close mutual support. Those familiar with the F-104 double-attack system and the Navy's loose-deuce tactics would notice many similarities in Six Pac. Obviously one week at a time does not an ace make, so the squadrons have their own ACT continuation training program. The pilots are required to fly a mandatory number of these missions each year. Because of the excellent support given by headquarters of ADC, the individual fighter squadrons are encouraged to make trips to various Naval fighter bases to participate in more dissimilar combat. The Navy squadrons also fly into the Sixes' home bases on occasion. The flying that results is aggressive, spirited, and educational. The mistakes made by both sides are lessons well learned in peace and won't be forgotten in combat.

I have yet to describe the actual flying characteristics of the airplane itself. In a word they are super. It is feather light in pitch responsiveness compared to the T-38. Without the external fuel tanks it is almost as responsive in roll as a T-38; with full external tanks the roll is slower and restricted to 100°/sec. The airplane has 752 KIAS "Q" limit, a Mach 2 restriction, and a skin temperature limit. It will easily go supersonic right on the deck or exceed the Mach 2 at altitude. During a recent TAC exercise two F-106s caught and successfully intercepted an F-111 going supersonic below 1,000 AGL (above ground level). Approach to a stall is very honest with light, medium, and heavy buffeting. Then lateral instability sets in causing the nose to wander in yaw. If the angle of attack is increased further beyond the critical, the adverse yaw induced by any aileron input will trigger a violent roll and pitch-up maneuver known as the post stall. The aircraft will oscillate about all three axes and if not recovered will likely enter a flat spin. Once established, the developed spin can be difficult to break. The rudder in the F-106 is extremely effective and in the high angle of attack regime is used to roll, thus avoiding the adverse yaw caused by aileron. The zero G maneuver to kill drag and prevent the stall is also effective in countering out-of-control flight. The F-106 accelerates beautifully, especially if already flying at a high indicated airspeed. By lighting the afterburner and pushing the nose over to zero G, the airspeed increases almost unbelievably. This airplane will go supersonic in a climb; it will even go super at high altitude in idle power by simply lowering the nose a few degrees. In fact if there is one complaint a "six" pilot has, it is that the airplane is difficult to slow down when you want it to.

Back in the landing pattern you fly initial at about 325 knots. The "break" is in a clean configuration rolling out on the downwind around 1,500 feet AGL, gear down, at about 240 knots. The final turn is flown at 200 knots in moderate buffet with a cross-check on the angle of attack. The pilot may opt to extend the speed brakes anywhere throughout the final turn or on approach. Power is gradually reduced after rolling out on final to transition from the final approach speed to the prior-to-flare speed. Then power is retarded to idle and the aircraft rate of descent is gently killed, causing airspeed to decrease another 10 knots to the touchdown speed. All three speeds are based on fuel remaining during landing. Once the wheels touch, the drag chute handle on the upper left side of the instrument panel is pulled and the drag chute deploys, causing a definite tug in the cockpit. The pilot raises the aircraft nose up to about 16° causing aerodynamic braking, being careful not to scrape the tailpipe. (That could cost him a case of beer to his crew chief.) When approaching 100 knots he lowers the nose to the runway and touches the button to engage the nosewheel steering. After turning off the active runway, he jettisons the drag chute by simply pushing the handle back in, and all the after-landing checks are then completed. The normal mission is two hours long, and unrefueled cross-countries have gone as much as three hours and fifteen minutes, covering over 1,600 N.M. Not bad for a fighter.

After 600 hours in the F-106 I still get a thrill walking up to her side. Airborne she's a thing of beauty to watch and a thrill to fly. Tactically the bulk of North American Air Defense responsibility still rests on her venerable old shoulders, and she always handles the job with style.

CAPT. PATRICK GAMBLE, the son of Major General Jack Gamble, is a squadron flight commander and instructor pilot at Grand Forks Air Force Base, North Dakota, with nearly 600 hours in the F-106.

F-111 Aardvark

PETER M. DUNN

THE Air Force has not formally named the F-111, but I suppose it really does not have to; as always, the crews have already done so. Although it deserves a more striking and sinister name to adequately reflect its excellent combat capability, those who fly the F-111 know it as the "Aardvark" (no doubt for its long, slender proboscis, so prominent at first sight). Never before has a flying machine been so highly publicized—for good or ill. The F-111 has been the subject of fierce political and technical controversy from conception to birth, and perhaps it is fitting that the most eloquent testimonials to the combat performance of the F-111 have come from the enemy.

A pilot or weapons system officer (WSO) coming from another fighter would notice several slight variances at first glance. The sheer size of the airplane is impressive; it grosses out at over 80,000 pounds with internal fuel only, compared to, say, an RF-4C's 52,000 pounds with three external fuel tanks. The F-111 may also look somewhat cluttered, what with wing high-lift devices (slats, flaps, rotating gloves) and pylons. The wings are high and set well back; only the outer halves of the wings (which seem to be set very far aft) can be seen from the cockpit. When one first sits in the cockpit the limited visibility is immediately noticeable. Because of the side-by-side seating arrangement the pilot must rely on the WSO to clear the sky visually on the right side, and occasionally cross-cockpit formation flying must be done. EB-66 pilots, who sat on the left and had no right seaters, will appreciate the problem. This matter is really not terribly important, since the F-111 works mainly alone, at night, on the deck, at flight parameters not approachable at present by other fighters.

A glance down the top of the aircraft will reveal a broad, flattish back, which generates a great deal of lift. A position about 100 yards behind an F-111 will give you a good view of this very wide dorsal area as it gently slopes down toward you. In the air, at forward wing sweeps and with gear down, the F-111 looks like a great mottled goose with long beak and high wings. But sweep the wings full aft and an incredible transformation occurs. The ugly duckling becomes a graceful, deadly, dartlike creature as it knifes through the sea of air—no frills and all business.

Since the F-111 has no ejection seat but employs an escape module, the usual detailed seat preflight is eliminated. Strapping in is a simple affair, and evidence of foresight and human engineering in the cockpit is readily apparent. It is a comfortable cockpit, and the airplane has often been referred to as the "Cadillac of fighters." There are actually places to stow charts, checklists, and flight publications.

Starting the engines is quite simple—and flexible. In addition to the usual pneumatic start, a starter cartridge can be used, and cross-bleed starts can be accomplished. Hot starts are almost unheard of. Unlike the J-79 engines in the F-4, which idled within very small permissible deviations from 66% rpm, the TF-30 can idle from 57 to 69% rpm.

Taxiing the F-111 is also a little different. The crew sits directly over the nosewheel, and the large main wheels are fairly close together. When making a tight turn one gets an impression of teetering. On takeoff, nosewheel liftoff averages about 142 knots. At Nellis Air Force Base, Nevada, where base altitude is over 1,800 feet and summer runway temperatures rise to 125°F and higher, takeoff distance is about 4,200 feet. Acceleration is fairly good for such a heavy aircraft. In the early A models maximum engine thrust is around 18,000 pounds per engine; later models have far more powerful engines in the 25,000-pound class. The stick is pulled back at rotation speed, but immediately after nose liftoff a forward stick motion may be required to arrest rotation of the aircraft. The pilot cannot snatch the gear up, as in other aircraft, because of the exceptionally long extension of the main gear struts. If the gear handle were raised while the wheels were still in contact with the runway, a pressure of 750 psi would be routed to the wheels for auto braking, and two blown tires would result.

The variable-sweep wings rotate on individual pivots and literally permit the pilot to redesign the aircraft in flight. The pivots are steel pins 8½ inches in diameter, set in a solid box which is the structural heart of the airplane. Wings extended to 16° provide a maximum surface area for greatest lift, permitting short takeoffs and landings. As speed increases and lift is converted to drag, wingspan and surface are reduced by sweeping the wings back to a maximum of 72.5°, where they lie tucked along the tail. No retrimming is necessary while sweeping the wings or changing speed, since the aircraft automatically and consistently trims itself to one G flight. As the wings move, the four inboard pylons also automatically readjust their alignment to remain streamlined at all times. The versatility and overlap of the system was dramatically illustrated by the four-ship "tiger formation" employed for displays by my old squadron: the leader flew with wings out at 26°, No. 2 and No. 3 set sweep of 45°, and the slot man was swept full aft at 72.5°. It was a pretty impressive sight as we flew over the field. The aircraft will slip through Mach 1 with about a 54° sweep; at Mach 1.7 or thereabouts the wings will be positioned to 72.5°, and the F-111 will punch through Mach 2 and higher. Because of its bulk, the F-111 makes a tremendous supersonic shock wave. Standing in a desert valley bombing range, I have seen the entire valley floor instantly erupt in a cloud of boiling dust, as if sharply struck by the flat of a giant hand, following a low-level supersonic bomb run.

The F-111, although a fighter, can carry an incredible bomb load. It has an internal weapons bay in addition to the wing-mounted pylons. A wide variety of ordnance can be loaded, including various sizes of general-

The F-111 in flight showing three different wing configurations—72.5°, 45°, and 16°.

purpose bombs, CBUs (chemical-biological units), rockets, and air-to-air missiles. A six-barrel 20 mm cannon is also installed.

After takeoff it seems to take a long time to clean the airplane up; the gear is raised, then the slats and flaps. Normal cruise wing sweep is 26°. The F-111 handles beautifully in the air. Like the gooney birds of Midway —which appear awkward and ungainly on the ground—it assumes a new personality when airborne, exuding grace and confidence as it glides over the earth. It is a very honest and responsive aircraft, and many pilots comment on the fact that there is no "dead" spot in the stick. A constant G response is commanded for a given amount of stick travel regardless of airspeed, altitude, or gross weight.

The range of the F-111 is astounding, especially for a flyer coming from another fighter. F-111s have crossed the Atlantic nonstop and without inflight refueling, on internal fuel only. At the time of this writing a Nellis crew has just returned from Pease Air Force Base, New Hampshire, a distance of about 2,250 miles. On the trip east they arrived over Pease after five hours and were still able to shoot several approaches and closed patterns before finally landing. This great range is due to another technical innovation in the F-111—the fan engine with five-stage afterburner.

I'm not sure if anyone really knows what the F-111's top speed really is. On my first flight in the F-111 we reached Mach 2 while climbing out from takeoff, still relatively heavy, and had to reduce speed only to keep from running out of the supersonic corridor. A nice turn was made at 1.8, and the aircraft performed exceedingly well (turns, rolls, etc.) while supersonic. It is designed to provide a stable bombing platform while supersonic on the deck, and it does this very well. The advertised top speed at altitude is Mach 2.5, or about 1,640 mph. For sustained high Mach operation a total temperature indicator is provided the aircrew. At very high speeds, when critical skin temperatures are approached, a red warning light comes on and commands the pilot to reduce speed. A digital readout will start to count down from 300 seconds. A "Total Temperature" lamp on the main caution panel will also light up. The pilot had better pull the power back at this time or structural damage could occur.

Should the crew be forced to abandon the aircraft, the only conscious effort required of either crew member is squeezing the ejection handle. Everything after that is completely automatic. Explosive charges sever the module from the aircraft. The module's rocket motor has lower and upper nozzles, and special sensors continually monitor aircraft speed and direct firing of the proper nozzle. At low speeds the lower, more powerful nozzle is fired, with a slight assist from the upper nozzle to maintain correct trajectory. G sensors and barostatic devices initiate deployment of the recovery parachute. The crew can select automatic chaff initiation at module separation to assist ground radars in detecting the bailout area. Center of gravity considerations are critical to ensure optimum escape attitude, and the weight differential between the crew members may not exceed 65 pounds. Even the thermos water bottles stowed above and behind each crew member must be filled and carried aboard, since they have an effect on proper module loading. A Nellis crew bailed out over the rugged terrain near the Grand Canyon not long ago. The module rolled down an incline for several hundred yards. The crew, strapped inside, emerged relatively untouched and stated that they might not have survived had a conventional ejection seat been used. My own experience in bailing out in a conventional rocket ejection seat over similar rugged country, with severe injury to the pilot, confirms this observation. The module will float if it lands in water, and extra flotation bags can be inflated; should high swells cause cabin flooding, the aircraft commander's control stick becomes a bilge pump. The crew can also sever the module from the aircraft while under water. Again, flotation bags inflate to help the module rise to the surface.

Have you ever watched a mallard duck come in for a landing? It comes in with neck taut, wings outstretched, and stubby legs close together and braced. That's the landing F-111 in a nutshell. Those who have landed aircraft like the F-101 and F-104 will appreciate the landing speed of the F-111. It will touch down within a few knots of nosewheel liftoff speed—somewhere around 140 knots, depending on landing weight and wing sweep (which will be 15° or 25°). The F-4 with the boundary layer control system approximates this. Initial approach speeds are standard—350 knots indicated. Pitchout is made with throttles at idle, 10–12 alpha units (an angle-of-attack measurement which is simpler to use than airspeed). Rollout on downwind is still at idle power, using what seems like a lengthy procedure to attain landing configuration. The main gear door is the speed brake. The gear is lowered first, followed by the slats, then flaps. Base turn is made with a bank angle of 30–40°, in contrast to the 50–70° of bank in some other fighters. Halfway through the turn on base, power is usually applied. With the fan engine, which accelerates relatively slowly, the pilot cannot afford to wait until he needs power to apply it in order to arrest sink rate. No matter how tightly he pitches out, once in landing configuration it is always possible to turn inside the pitch.

The final approach is with power on, holding 10 alpha. Ground effect is experienced upon approaching the overrun, which tends to shallow out the angle of attack. This is countered by applying slight back stick, which is definitely not a flare or roundout. As soon as touchdown is achieved and the engines retarded to idle, wing spoilers rise to kill wing lift and assist in slowing the aircraft. The F-111 has no drag chute, but braking qualities are so excellent that short field landings are no problem. The tires are big, and maintenance gets ten times more landings out of these tires than from those on any other fighters.

To those with experience in high-speed low-level flight, one thing that is instantly noticeable is the steady, granitelike ride. Other fighters flying within similar low-level parameters ride "hard"—the aircraft is striving hard and the ride is bumpy in any sort of unstable air. The F-111 glides through the Mach at low level so easily that the crew would never know the difference were it not for the Mach indicator. The reason for this is the stability augmentation system. This flight control system is unique in that it is self-adaptive. Heretofore, the only other aircraft to possess this feature was the X-15. Triple-redundant pitch, roll, and yaw circuits constantly compensate for deviations in aircraft motion; and computer-commanded corrections are performed before the crew is aware of any possible turbulence or gusting. The result is one of the most solid, stable rides imaginable.

The TFR (terrain-following radar) is another system that makes this airplane unusual. With the deployment of the 474th Tactical Fighter Wing to Southeast Asia in September 1972, the United States finally had a full-time, credible night low-level strike capability. Terrain-following radar systems were not new; *automatic* TFR systems were. The missions flown by the 474th over North Vietnam could not have been accomplished manually. The crew can select a variety of altitudes as well as kinds of ride desired: a three-position switch directs a soft, medium, or hard ride. Soft ride programs a gentle pull-up over high ground; hard ride brings the aircraft closer to terrain before initiating a steeper pull-up; in hard ride the descent commands up to a zero G pushover. The TFR also has a situation mode, which permits the crew to fly around peaks rather than over them, and a ground-mapping mode which does what the name implies. One can also make excellent fixed-angle bomb runs with the ground-mapping mode of the TFR, which provides a backup in case the attack radar system (ARS) is lost. The TFR system is dual channel; should the operating system fail, another identical system will automatically take over. If a malfunction occurs anywhere in the system, fail-safe circuits will command an immediate and shuddering pull-up.

Both ground and airborne TFR checks are performed to test the radars and the fail-safe circuits. The aircraft will automatically descend on command, hands off, at a rate of about 10,000 feet per minute. At 5,000 feet above ground level the radar altimeter will identify the earth's surface, and the rate of descent will increase noticeably until just prior to the preselected altitude where a smooth level-off is automatically accomplished. The stick will not move as the aircraft climbs and descends over mountain and valley; the climb and dive commands are sent directly from the TFR computer to the pitch channel of the flight control system. Occasionally it may be necessary to apply power as a particularly steep mountain is approached. In the inky blackness of night it is initially unnerving to look out and see the black hulks of mountains slide by above you as the aircraft settles into a valley.

The weapons system officer backs up the TFR with the big ARS and continuously alerts the pilot to the terrain picture ahead. The ARS has outstanding resolution. Its frequency agility characteristic does two important things for the operator: by continuously and automatically shifting frequencies it approaches optimum reflectivity of the wide variety of materials swept by the radar and provides antijamming function as well. After using equipment like this I could never think of returning to other aircraft I've flown—such as the B-52, EB-66, and RF-4C—much as I enjoyed them all.

As the target is approached, the WSO punches a button that recalls target coordinates set into the computer before flight. The radar cross hairs automatically reach out and settle on the target, and the inertial navigation system is generally so good that the usual problem of last-minute radar scope interpretation is eliminated. If the target is a "no-show," offset bombing capability is available.

The TFR system will keep the aircraft at the desired bombing altitude. However, if the BCU (ballistics computer unit) is being used, delivery parameters are not critical; the BCU will constantly and automatically adjust ballistics for changes in heading, airspeed, and altitude until bombs away. Should the BCU fail, manual ballistics inserted into the system before flight can be instantly used. F-111 crews still debate whether the auto bomb mode using the BCU is as accurate as trail bomb using manual ballistics; it's a moot point, since the bombing circular error averages in both are so good. Visual lay-down nuclear bombing attacks can be made at 200 feet and 520 knots minimum airspeed, using the pilot's lead computing optical sight.

While aircrews have always been totally mystified at the bad press the F-111 has received, the aircraft finally began to receive some well-earned praise as a result of the Linebacker I and II campaigns—the air offensives over North Vietnam in 1972. Night after night the F-111s took off from Takhli Royal Thai Air Force Base, Thailand, armed with Mark 82 500-pound bombs or Mark 84 2,000-pound general-purpose bombs, descended over Laos to terrain-following altitudes, flew at low altitudes as far as the northeast railroad, delivered their ordnance, and returned to Laos at low altitudes before climbing out for home. Well over an hour was spent at very low altitudes and high speeds, and the entire mission from start to finish was flown with internal fuel only and no inflight refueling. No other fighter in the world can even approximate this performance. Medium-altitude missions were flown against enemy forces in Laos and against the supply trails along the panhandle, and the great accuracy of the radar bombing systems repeatedly broke the backs of Communist attacks. The legendary General Vang Pao, the Laotian Lawrence, presented the 474th Tactical Fighter Wing with a trophy AK-47 rifle as an expression of thanks. Captured North Vietnamese troops referred to F-111s as "whispering death."

On days when solid undercast would normally have prevented fighter strikes on enemy forces, we rendezvoused with flights of F-4 or A-7 aircraft that released their ordnance on command of the F-111, which was bombing by radar. This technique of pathfinder bombing proved to be very valuable and was employed night and day. While the B-52s rightly earned great praise for their part in the final December blitz over North Vietnam, it was the F-111 aircraft which—singly and largely unheralded—struck the enemy MIG airfields, SAM (surface-to-air missile) and gun sites, and other threats minutes before the big bombers appeared on the scene and directly contributed to minimizing B-52 losses.

It is ironic indeed that it was the North Vietnamese themselves who did a great deal to build the legend that is growing around this airplane. Communist air defense forces never succeeded in solving the problem of detecting intruding F-111s. POWs returning from Hanoi told of Communist target areas sounding the all clear after strikes by other U.S. aircraft, only to be completely surprised minutes later by lone F-111s roaring over and attacking their targets. One of the Nellis crews, who was hit by a "golden BB" in December, told of the Communist prison guard who came up to him and said, "You F-111." Then making a flat horizontal sweeping motion with the palm of his hand, he shook his head in admiration and said, "Whoosh." An amazing compliment by the enemy. I don't think I can improve on that.

MAJ. PETER M. DUNN has had three tours in Southeast Asia, including more than 100 missions over North Vietnam. He has flown combat in the EB-66 and the F-111. He recently received the M.A. degree in history from the University of Nevada.

CG-4A Glider

ARTHUR J. THOMAS

SOAR to Victory on the Silent Wings of a Glider/ Become a Glider Pilot in the U.S. Army Air Corps. Thus read the USAAF recruiting pamphlet released in the spring of 1942. That we played a part in the victory has been established. Our capability for "soaring to victory," however, left much to be desired.

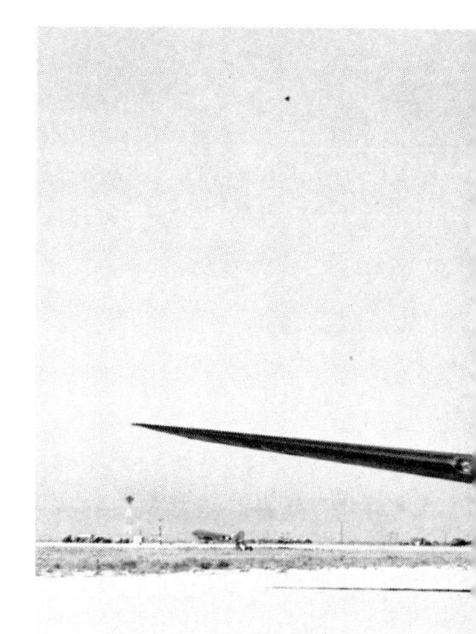

Generally, if in the spring of 1942 you were between the ages of 18 and 35, could walk and talk, and were warm, you qualified as a glider pilot candidate. But not in my case! Having initially been rejected for being six pounds underweight, I ate 30 cents worth of bananas and drank lots of water before my next examination. When told that I was still underweight, I could no longer hold the load and preceeded to dirty up the gymnasium floor where the physicals were being held. The kindly old physician smiled and said, "Sonny, if you want it that badly, you're in!"

The CG-4A—designated Glider, Heavy Transport—was strictly a utility glider with little or none of the soaring capabilities attributed to its little sister, the high-performance sailplane. With an aspect ratio of 8.2 and a sink rate approaching 950 feet per minute at 100 mph, there was only one way for the CG-4A to go after tow release—down!

Towline being attached to a glider, 1943.

A towed glider leaving the ground.

A C-53 tug and glider taking off. The glider leaves the ground first.

Gliders, now flying free, start to peel off and swoop down to a fast landing on any patch of level ground.

When first introduced to the CG-4A at South Plains Army Air Field, Lubbock, Texas, in mid-1943, I was immediately impressed in two ways. First, it was the largest aircraft most of us had ever seen; secondly, if not the largest, it had to be the ugliest!

The CG-4A, designed to be used for troop and cargo transport, was a strut-braced high-wing cabin monoplane. It had a wing span of 83 feet 8 inches and a wing area of approximately 852 square feet. The overall length was 48 feet 3 inches. Empty weight was 3,089 pounds; with a useful load of 3,711 pounds total gross weight was 6,800 pounds. The nose could be opened upward; when the glider was equipped with tactical landing gear, a jeep could be driven inside and securely fastened for transport in a very few minutes. Pilot and copilot were seated side by side. The seating arrangement along the sides of the aisle accommodated 13 fully equipped soldiers. Entrance doors on the right and left of the fuselage aft of the wing were sufficiently wide for a fully armed man to walk through with ease. Emergency exits on each side of the fuselage were located under the wings. Visibility was generally good for the pilot and copilot, and there were six round observation windows along each side of the fuselage. The tech manual stated: "These windows are to help minimize airsickness on the part of the airborne troops; . . . men aft of the center of gravity tend to become airsick very easily." There were two racks of sanitary containers in the ship for this possibility.

Wing construction was conventional for that time—two-spar wood construction, fabric covered, and built in four sections for quick disassembly. The wing planform was straight with elliptical tips and little or no dihedral. Fuselage construction, square in cross section, was of welded steel tubing with a plywood honeycomb floor and fabric cover. One peculiarity was in the landing gear: the takeoff gear was to be jettisoned after leaving the ground and the landing was to be made on wooden skids under each side of the belly. On gliders used for training purposes a more permanent landing gear was added, with brakes and shock absorbers; but in the original design of the glider the added strain of the training gear was not included in the fuselage structure, so it was quite easy to pull the landing gear loose on rough landings. The tech manual noted that "this weakness should be kept in mind and rough landings should be prevented as much as possible."

The aircraft had dual-control wheels arranged side by side, and it could be trimmed in respect to all three axes with three separate trim tab controls above and between the pilot and copilot seats. Instruments consisted of an airspeed indicator, a sensitive altimeter, bank and turn indicator, and rate of climb indicator; a few had a two-way radio, which was generally not in operating condition.

Another unique feature of the CG-4A was the spoilers. With this device the pilot was able to kill off a large percentage of the lift created by the modified Clark-Y airfoil. A lever was located on the outboard side of each seat in the cockpit, so either the pilot or the copilot could activate the spoilers. Use of the spoilers could increase the rate of descent from a normal 950 feet per minute at 100 mph to as much as 1,600 feet per minute. Thus the glider pilot soon learned to plan all approaches on the long or high side so that in the final moments before touchdown the spoilers could be utilized to put the glider on the intended spot.

The CG-4A was to be flown not more than 25° up, 20° down, or

20° to the right or left of the extended longitudinal axis of the tow ship. Maximum indicated airspeed was placarded at 120 mph. Minimum load was a pilot, copilot, and 600 pounds of ballast—300 pounds located immediately behind each pilot seat.

As was standard in nearly all training programs of the day, before the student pilot began his transition flying he was required to spend at least one hour of familiarization in the cockpit of the CG-4A. We used gliders grounded for repairs to learn the location of the trim tabs, and their action when turned to the right or left was memorized. Blindfolded, we had to demonstrate to the instructor that we could locate the airspeed indicator and altimeter.

During this period we were impressed with the necessity for promptness in checking out parachutes and being in the assigned gliders as soon as possible after receiving our assignments for the day. In spite of the fact that we had spent 13 months to complete 10 weeks of training up to this point, we were informed that time was not expendable and every minute of delay was holding up the training program.

At last the big day arrived! We were terribly excited at the prospect of finally flying the glider that was to be our combat airplane. Comfortable seating in the CG-4A for the pilot depended to a great extent on how large he was and how many pillows were available. The seat itself was not adjustable, either up and down or fore and aft. After finding a reasonably comfortable position, probably the first thing we noted was the extreme cockpit roominess. Never before had we flown in an airplane where two pilots sat side by side with room between for another pilot, and off our outside elbows there was at least 12–14 inches to the outside wall of the cockpit.

Although our span was almost as large as the Lockheed Lodestar tow plane, our pre-takeoff checklist was extremely simple: "Control checks off and securely fastened, pitot tube uncovered, controls checked for full movement, read the form 1-A status of the aircraft, safety belt fastened, 300-pound ballast in place and properly fastened, trim tabs set to neutral, meter pin flush in the towrope release mechanism, altimeter set, brakes off, ailerons in neutral position." When this had been accomplished, the pilot gave the signal to the ground crewman, who in turn relayed it to the tow plane, and the Lodestar started to take up the slack in the rope.

Initially the control wheel was held in the full back position to apply up elevator, so if the tow plane took up the rope slack too quickly there would be some assistance in keeping the glider from nosing over and riding on the skids. The towline fastening on the glider was mounted high on the nose, and there was quite a tendency for the glider to nose over on the initial pull of the tow plane. As the glider began to move, the wheel was moved gently forward until the glider was in level position, rolling on the landing gear. Enough rudder was used to keep the glider directly behind the tow ship; when a 60 mph airspeed was reached, the wheel was gently eased back until the glider was approximately 20 feet above the runway. At this point it was necessary to ease the wheel forward so that the glider was in a slight diving attitude to put a slack in the towline, thus allowing the tow plane to leave the runway. After the tow plane was airborne the glider was flown level until the tow plane came up to its proper position, which was just below that of the glider. If the glider was flown too high immediately after takeoff, the tow ship was unable to leave the runway. Takeoff commenced with the elevator trim tabs in a moderately nose-down position. As the glider gained airspeed there was an appreciable nose trim effect. The glider student was cautioned, however, to devote his undivided attention to keeping proper tow position and to signal the copilot or instructor to trim the nose or wings immediately after takeoff if that were desirable. A more experienced glider pilot was able to make the takeoff with one hand and trim the aircraft with the other.

Techniques for takeoff were slightly different when the glider was fully loaded. The glider pilot had to bear in mind that the tow ship was dragging 3½ tons of weight, in addition to the full load of the tow ship itself, and needed every assistance. We were cautioned not to increase drag by climbing too fast during the early stages but to wait until the tow ship had accelerated to its approximate liftoff speed; then by increasing the angle of attack we slowly transferred the weight from the landing gear to the wing so that the glider left the ground at approximately the same time as the tow plane.

In anticipation of problems due to our lack of experience in flying aircraft with side-by-side seating, the tech manual cautioned pilots that they were sitting approximately 18 inches to the left of the longitudinal axis of the glider and hence the same distance to the left of the point where the towrope connected. "By leaning to the right and sighting along the towrope the glider student can easily see if he is lined up with the center of the tow ship fuselage; if not, he can correct his position accordingly." We found that this maneuver of leaning over toward the center of the glider in an attempt to line up the towrope with the tow aircraft increased the chances of vertigo, particularly during night flying.

Danger of taking off in a low tow position was emphasized. "Added drag of the prop wash could on occasion cause a towrope failure. On the takeoff the [glider] pilot should always be ready to release the towrope in the event one of the tow ship's motors failed or if the tow ship encountered difficulty leaving the runway." If the towrope were to break, the procedure was immediate release, to prevent the dragging rope from catching on obstructions on the ground. The only path left for the glider pilot in such an emergency was to make the best possible landing. If a glider was flown low enough to get into the prop wash during takeoff, it was difficult to control and much additional strain was placed on the towrope. Flown too high, the towrope became taut and exerted an upper pull on the tow ship's tail. The best position to fly was that which maintained constant sag in the towrope and constant airspeed.

The bank and turn indicator needle was the only cockpit indication of a good towing position. The needle was centered with rudder, the ball centered with aileron, and any pressures relieved by proper trimming. Occasionally a wing became so heavy that slight pressure would be required on the opposite aileron to maintain proper attitude even with full trim corrections. In smooth air light pressure on the controls was all that was required; the prime difficulty of beginning students was overcontrolling. The cargo glider tended to oscillate while on tow; this characteristic was not experienced in the sailplanes and other light gliders we had previously flown. We soon learned that the tendency to overcorrect would result in an increasing oscillation, and we learned to pick up the low wing with the opposite rudder and use as little aileron as possible. To stop the oscillation after it had started, slight cross-controlling was necessary. This was

The entire pilot's compartment of the glider lifted on hinges for loading a jeep.

almost identical to the corrective action taken today to stop the "Dutch roll" of the Boeing 707. In moderate turbulence the tow plane and glider bounced around considerably, and heavy pressure and large control movements were required to make the glider respond when the air was gusty. Keeping the glider in proper tow position required undivided attention on the part of the glider pilot, and on tows of longer than half an hour it was recommended that the copilot take over for a few minutes to give the pilot a chance to rest his eyes and look around.

Turns presented no particular problem as long as the pilot could clearly see the tow plane. As the tow plane started a bank for a turn, the glider pilot did likewise, matching the angle of bank observed. Very little control pressure was required to bank the glider; when the desired bank had been accomplished, a slight pressure in the opposite direction was required to prevent overbanking. In climbs a glider pilot maintained his position slightly above the tow plane, and during descent moderate use of the spoilers dissipated altitude without excessive diving.

The most crucial thing a glider pilot had to learn—and learn well—was the determination of the tow release point. The critical factors involved in this decision were altitude, surface winds, and the path of the tow plane during the final moments.

The CG-4A had a gliding ratio of 9.25 in calm air at 100 mph, but it covered well over 12 feet forward for every foot lost at our normal 70 mph glide. Indication of surface winds can be quite misleading. As is well known, a wind velocity of 20–30 miles an hour on the ground can be considerably higher at altitude. In stronger winds glide speed was increased from the normal 70 mph to 100 mph in order to cover any appreciable distance over the ground. At 100 mph the rate of descent approached 950 feet per minute. In these conditions the glide ratio was reduced to as little as 4–5 feet of forward distance to every foot of loss of altitude. A pilot cutting loose downwind from the field in winds of high velocity had very little opportunity to plan an approach and land in the designated area. If the tow plane failed to put the glider in the proper position on the upwind side at the prearranged altitude for release, the glider pilot could elect to stay on tow until a position was attained from which he could make a safe landing in the designated area. Except in an emergency, the glider pilot always made the tow release decision.

Prior to release, the glider was pulled up gently to slightly above the normal tow position and all slack taken out of the towrope. The glider was then put into a moderate dive to create slack for releasing. Excessive speed was used to gain additional altitude if required. As the airspeed settled down to approximately 70 mph, trim tabs were adjusted so that the glider would fly "hands off."

Training maneuvers consisted of coordination exercises (rolling the aircraft about its axis with the nose on the horizon). The practice of stalls involved a very gentle entry with the ailerons in a neutral position. After the nose dropped below the horizon, it was necessary to pull the wheel gently back again to establish a normal glide speed. Much time was devoted to the practice of needle-width 360° turns at a constant speed of 70 mph. However, it should be pointed out that a large radius was necessary to make a needle-width turn and that the loss of altitude was considerable. If this type of turn was used in a landing pattern, it was extremely difficult to plan a rectangular approach from a key altitude. This was compounded by the fact that there was not time to observe the traffic and judge the velocity of the wind while on the base leg. Three-needle-width turns were far more practical. In a three-needle-width turn at 70 mph altitude loss approximated 400 feet in 360° of turn or 100 feet in a 90° turn. Therefore, in traffic patterns steep coordinated turns were used. The lazy-8 maneuver in a glider was not too different from the lazy-8 in most other airplanes. At 90–100 mph the glider was put into a 20° bank toward the checkpoint, and the nose lifted in a coordinated climbing turn. As a near-stall condition was reached at the top of the 8, the nose was eased through the checkpoint; during the downward swing almost full aileron travel was required to maintain the proper altitude, and this pressure gradually eased off as the glider gained the speed necessary for the second half of the 8. This was the only maneuver the glider was stressed for other than steep turns and gentle stalls.

Under no condition was a cargo glider to be allowed to spin or get the nose high enough for it to "whip stall." We did find later in the overseas limited-supervision environment that the CG-4A would perform a beautiful loop. If executed immediately after a tow release, two loops could be performed with practically no loss of altitude. During a contest among unemployed glider pilots at Guidonia Airfield in Italy a record of 15 loops was accomplished off a high-speed tow from a release point some 3,500 feet above the runway. The holder of this dubious honor did contact the ground on the final pullout, tore off the landing gear, and caused one wing to collapse. In addition his landing roll was somewhat shortened.

The normal landing pattern was a rectangular side approach; the

Interior view of the CG-4A glider.

glider entered downwind at 1,200 feet, passed abeam of the landing spot at 1,000 feet, turned onto the base leg at 800 feet, and completed the final approach turn at 400 feet. This was entirely theoretical; the size of the field, velocity of the wind, and the load carried were the ultimate deciding factors. On days with a wind velocity of more than 20 mph, the base leg was made just outside the landing area, the approach purposely high, with spoilers used during final approach. Student pilots were taught forward slips, but this was considered an emergency maneuver; spoilers were preferred on both the base and final approach. Final approach speed (well over stalling speed) ran 70–90 mph, depending on the load. Touchdown was approximately 60 mph. The CG-4A fully loaded was never glided at less than 80 mph, and a speed around 90 was preferred.

Landings from a 200-foot-altitude tow release both straight ahead and with a 90° turn into final approach were practiced, but only after the student pilot had at least three hours of experience in the airplane.

A third type of approach, known as the "dive approach," was taught as a result of experience in the British heavy glider training program. It was designated as a measure to avoid fire from enemy ground defenses. In this approach the glider peeled off from an altitude of 1,000–2,000 feet and dived at a predetermined spot on the ground, as much as a mile from the intended landing point. Before diving the pilot made a mental picture of the intended flight path. After pulling out of the dive as close to the ground as possible, the pilot hedgehopped over and around obstructions until he arrived "unexpectedly" at the landing zone. This approach—though considered very effective—allowed very little margin for pilot error in estimating wind strength, flight path, and excessive speed necessary.

No discussion of the approaches of the CG-4A would be complete without some mention of the "Curry glide" (named after Colonel Curry who was its greatest exponent). Actually it should have been called the "Curry mush." Colonel Curry's objective was to land the glider with the shortest possible landing roll after touchdown; thus the Curry glide was a minimum airspeed approach. Because of the positioning of the pitot tube on the CG-4A, the airspeed indicator was of little value on this approach; when it was properly accomplished, the airspeed indications fluctuated quite widely. The best point of reference the pilot had was the bottom surface of the wing out near the wing tip. When this surface indicated a positive angle of attack as related to the horizon beyond, he was approaching the proper attitude. This actually produced a flight condition of riding just on the burble of the approaching stall. The burble felt in the ailerons was probably the best indication of the proper glide speed. The maneuver was quite successful in reducing the amount of ground run. The CG-4A in this configuration could be landed over a 50-feet obstacle and stopped with less than 300 feet of ground roll without use of wheel brakes. Unfortunately, since the rate of sink was around 1,500 feet per minute, quite often the gear collapsed on touchdown. In this case, landing roll was considerably shortened.

Perhaps the most interesting and exciting stage of training for the glider pilot was the "night blitz landings." These were made under blackout conditions with a low-altitude release at 200 feet on a base leg followed by a 90° turn to final. The only reference point out in that big black void of a field was a smudge pot sitting on the ground. This maneuver was performed with as many as 20–25 gliders which arrived at the tow release point at intervals of approximately 30 seconds. The idea was to make your turn, line up with the light on the ground, and park the aircraft so that your left wing tip was over the smudge pot. The copilot immediately jumped out of his seat, ran out the left rear door, picked up the pot, ran beind the glider, and placed the pot 15 feet outboard of the right wing tip. Thus the next aircraft in line would have a designated parking position. It was not unusual for the pilot turning final and lining up on the smudge pot to see the light all of a sudden jump up and follow an erratic course approximately 110 feet to the right. Taking this element of surprise into his mental calculations he readjusted his estimate of his final destination and realigned the glider on final approach so that he could wind up with the light under his left wing tip. Shortly after touchdown, during the landing roll, he might again see the light picked up and moved to the right. Not infrequently after an evening of this maneuver, the glider program shut down for a day or two so that maintenance could catch up on their repair work.

The only emergency precedure discussed at any length in regard to glider flying concerned an error in judgment on the part of the pilot. From the Cessna-produced tech manual dated December 17, 1942:

> If the pilot sees that he made an error in judgment, the first consideration is to save the equipment and thereby prevent injury to himself and his passengers. In a strong headwind the speed of the glider must be increased to 100 to 120 miles per hour to make any headway over the ground. If it is evident that the glider will hit a fence or other obstruction at the normal gliding speed, the speed should be increased by pointing the nose down at the top of the obstruction and a few seconds before reaching it pulling the wheel back gently and zooming over. It is possible to lift the glider from 50 to 100 feet in this manner with an airspeed of 100 miles an hour. Do not fly along at 60 miles and guess whether or not the glider will clear the obstruction. Put the nose on the object and make certain that it will clear by lifting over it at the proper time.

Surely the Cessna writers had good intentions, but I have yet to see or hear of a case where this emergency procedure actually succeeded. An error in judgment invariably resulted in a horizontal fence, a demolished outhouse, or a bashed-in chicken coop as well as a very sick glider. [I used to do this with the Cessna Crane in 1944; it was a new maneuver to the RCAF!—Editor]

A typical cargo glider combat mission took place on August 15, 1944, when some 75 tow planes and their gliders left Rosignano Air Field just west of Rome at 3:30 in the afternoon for the invasion of southern France. A low altitude was flown en route to preclude detection by enemy radar, which had recently been installed in the Genoa area. Flight time from Rosignano to the landing area in southern France was some 3 hours and 15 minutes. Arrival time over the southern coast of France was planned to allow one hour of daylight in order to make our landing, discharge our load, and set up a perimeter defense in enemy-held territory for the night.

Of the 75 gliders that departed on this mission all but two made it to the area of the designated landing zones. One turned back because somebody had failed to remove the down lock pins in the C-47 tow plane undercarriage. The other was literally blown out of the sky shortly after we passed checkpoint Orbitello. It was later ascertained that this glider was carrying ten drums of gasoline destined to be used in jeeps which were carried in several of the gliders.

Upon our arrival in the landing area just north and east of Frejus, France, visibility was extremely poor because of smoke from fires created by "softening up" fighter and bomber attacks, which had taken place in the area during the day. The landing area (according to intelligence reports at our premission briefing) was large, perfectly clear, and almost level. The fields designated for our landings had, however, unbeknown to the briefers, been planted in vineyards and a peach orchard. Choosing the lesser of two evils, the first 15 or 20 gliders landed in the vineyards, which offered the least hazard to a safe landing. Those of us who were farther back in line took the peach orchard. The last few gliders had little choice of a decent landing area but did the best they could, with some rather disastrous results. The intelligence information must have been somewhat outdated!

The glider pilots had been admonished with the threat that any pilot who did not make a successful landing and leave the glider in a recoverable condition would surely sign a statement of charges for the same. An estimated 75 percent of the gliders were completely demolished. We soon found that it would be to our advantage to burn the gliders, after unloading their contents, to deprive enemy snipers of their protective cover. This we did, but I have not yet paid the charges.

The glider payloads, for the most part delivered in good operable condition, included miniature bulldozers, gasoline, ammunition, airborne troopers, and—of all things—a chapel organ, hymnals, and a Red Cross doughnut-making machine. Not faring so well, however, were the pilots themselves. Multiple fractures of the lower extremities were most numerous. If only somebody had told us to place our feet up on the instrument panel prior to mowing down a row of young peach trees! The fabric-covered ⅜-inch plywood beneath our feet offered little protection.

The glider pilot's job after he got on the ground was that of an infantryman. During our long, drawn-out training program we had been qualified in the use of most of the armament of the foot soldier; it was not at all unusual during the early hours of that invasion to see glider pilots firing bazookas, 75 mm pack howitzers, 60 mm mortars, and .50-caliber air-cooled machine guns.

The CG-4A glider was a big flying machine—an ugly flying machine; it was uncomfortable, and the missions were hazardous. If ever the statement "I wouldn't swap the experience for a million dollars nor do it again for another million dollars" was appropriate, it certainly applies here.

The author beside the wreckage of his glider in France in 1944.

LT. COL. ARTHUR J. THOMAS, a glider pilot in World War II, served as an all-weather radar-intercept observer and directed a test program for an electronic aerial geodetic survey system before retiring from the USAF in 1971. He is currently a student in landscape architecture at Kansas State University and maintains an active status in civilian flying.

O-2A Super Skymaster

TIMOTHY KLINE

A HIGH-WING, all-metal aircraft with retractable tricycle landing gear, the O-2A possessed uniquely designed centerline mounted twin engines—one on the nose and one between the twin tail booms. Cleverly eliminating the often hazardous asymmetrical thrust problems of conventional twin-engine aircraft, the plane provided excellent handling characteristics throughout its speed range of 80–200 mph. A far cry from the "fork-tailed devil" of World War II fame (the P-38), this twin-boom, push-pull prop plane endeared itself to pilots in the low and slow combat environment of Southeast Asia. Known affectionately and unofficially as the "Oscar Deuce," it acquired less respectable titles with remarkable ease. Forward Air Controllers (FACs) who labeled it "Oscar Pig" and "Oscar Douce" bemoaned its sluggish performance, poor visibility, and lack of power. In a climb the two 210 hp Continentals strained for altitude. In a dive the heavily laden craft (maximum gross weight 4,850 pounds) threatened to overspeed the props. Still, all things considered, few FACs complained about the plane's best feature—the second engine.

Twice in my experience that other engine enabled me to bring the bird home in appropriate style. Both times I had been conducting visual reconnaissance over heavy jungle with no place below me suitable for a forced landing; but for a second chance my plane and I might have been converted into a decorative ornament for the high branches of the ominous trees which beckoned below. On one of these occasions I had thrown a rod on the rear engine. More powerful for mysterious reasons relating to aerodynamics and airflow, it was generally conceded to be the wrong one to lose if you had the choice. There were persistent rumors that without a rear engine the O-2 would be unable to climb, might even be unable to hold its own altitude, and might possibly give you a nice controlled glide eventually bringing man and machine to an unwelcome greeting with terra firma. I am happy to relate that you can maintain altitude with only a front engine operating at full throttle. Of course I had to close the small cowl flaps on either side of the rear engine and below the forward engine. I had, in addition, the unpleasant task of dropping my two rocket pods and

CESSNA

The O-2A in flight from the factory. The O-2B was taken off the Cessna shelf in 1966 and sent directly to Vietnam with minimal military conversion.

fourteen rockets over enemy territory, to reduce the drag and to streamline things a bit. Fortunately the terrain below me was the flat land of sea level swamps near Saigon. Had I been over the rugged mountains of I or II Corps, my tale might not have ended so propitiously.

Originally built by Cessna as a "doctor's airplane" and designated the 337 Super Skymaster, the O-2 was packed with 600 pounds of UHF, VHF, and FM radios; painted gray and white; fitted with four pylons for rockets, flares, and even a set of 7.62 mm miniguns (which were apparently never used in anger); and then sent off to war with minimal fanfare. Its primary virtues—as a replacement for Cessna's older FAC aircraft the O-1 Bird Dog—were twin engines, higher cruising speeds, and the capability of carrying more rockets (especially important for putting in multiple air strikes or even a single strike where high winds might blow the smoke away too quickly, requiring frequent marking passes by the FAC). For these beneficial features it sacrificed visibility, ruggedness, and the ability to operate off grass strips. It has always seemed to me that the O-2 was simply an uneasy compromise between the low-cost but limited Bird Dog and the high-priced but far more talented Bronco (OV-10).

In many ways the O-2 reminded me of a dwarfed scale model of some real airplane. The wing pylons were tiny, the main wheels were small black orbs, and the plane was built low to the ground. One day I watched four O-2s taxi out for takeoff and line up behind an AC-119 gunship. The collective group gave the appearance of four ducklings following mama to the lake.

While the aircraft was indescribably ungainly on the ground, it was almost sleek and swift-looking in flight; the main problem was getting it airborne. After entering through the right-hand door you crawled across the seat gingerly, avoiding the radios and instrument panel. Because of an

The author pointing out characteristics of his O-2A.

uncomfortably long takeoff roll (anywhere from 1,000 to 3,500 feet), I was always careful to line up with plenty of runway ahead; when the plane was loaded with full rockets and flares, the takeoff process could be lengthy. Once free of earth's friction the O-2 behaved distinctively. When the tiny gear handle was placed up, a remarkable thing would happen: the nose gear behaved normally; but the main wheels, after starting up quite regularly, would stop abruptly halfway through the procedure and rotate fully flat into the windstream, causing the airframe to shudder in protest and the airspeed indicator to hesitate as if speed brakes had been applied. After half a heartbeat the main wheels would resume their upward movement and tuck neatly below the aft engine. Normal climb could then be resumed. From the vantage point of a ground observer it reminded me of a great gander getting aloft—with webbed feet first dangling flat and back, then knees up and finally into the up-and-locked position somewhere in the tail feathers.

The O-2 will never find service in the high-spirited stable of the Thunderbirds, nor will it be lauded by the Air Force as the final answer to the problematical needs of forward air control. But it did perform well in skilled hands. It seated two side by side, or four with passenger seats added, and possessed two sets of controls; but I'm convinced it was the most difficult FAC aircraft for controlling air strikes. Visibility from the left side of the cockpit was so bad that most jocks found themselves invariably in left turns favoring the nearest window. To improve vision Cessna had cut a window in the lower right door and one just forward in the right-hand wall. Two more windows had been cut into the roof. Despite these modifications, most FACs were seen circling left over target areas.

Then there was the not inconsiderable aggravation caused by the control wheel. Not a bad fixture in an executive's cross-country aircraft, it was out of place in the gyrating world of the constantly turning, climbing, and diving FAC. To keep the fighters, friendlies, and target in sight in a plane with zero visibility to the rear (there was an engine in the way) and precious few windows while wheeling, talking, and setting up armament switches was no mean task. The O-2 driver had his hands full controlling a strike; during these hectic moments a stick, a turboprop, and a bubble canopy would have been welcomed.

To its credit I must admit the O-2 was reliable and sturdier than I had expected. Even the tinker-toy landing gear system rarely caused grief. The bird could get to distant targets more quickly than the O-1, preventing unneccessary frustration for fighter pilots, but its vaunted speed advantage was certainly no quantum jump. The O-2 cruised at 160 mph maximum, with normal cruise of nearly 140 under combat loads; the O-1 cruising speed was 85–90 mph.

Most effective at night, with a lusty roar and an exceptionally fine instrument panel, the smooth-cruising aircraft loaded with flares and rockets could be remarkably potent. I once ferried an O-2 to the people at Pleiku who did most of their business at night over the Ho Chi Minh trail. Their O-2s were painted solid black and looked quite lethal in the revetments.

Having flown the F-4C for four years I was pleasantly surprised to find the O-2A equipped with a very similar gunsight. Basically a noncomputing, pipper-and-ring projecting type with manual mil adjustment, it made a handsome addition to the glare shield of the left instrument panel. Immediately beside it were rocker-type arming switches. I soon discovered the O-2 was a stable platform for rocket firing and, once I had adjusted to the parallax problem of firing from a side-by-side cockpit, was able to fire with good accuracy. Toward the end of my tour, while checking out an instructor pilot in a free fire zone, we came upon an enemy soldier paddling surreptitiously along a tributary of the Mekong. We attempted some single shots with the few rockets we had left in the tubes and hit fairly close to his sampan. The enemy reacted by beaching his small sampan, uncovering an AK-7, and returning our fire. While unable to hit the Vietcong soldier standing at the water's edge, we probably succeeded in unsettling him. A rocket failing to hit its target still makes a nerve-shattering crash as it breaks the sound barrier prior to impact. The 2.75-inch rockets with phosphorus warheads can be lethal if they hit close enough, and having witnessed many aerial demonstrations of target marking, I can attest to their aural ferocity.

One aspect of flying the O-2 was particularly strange. Although many modifications had been made to adapt the airplane to its combat role, one item was conspicuously overlooked by the Cessna engineers. The seats were flimsy, without the slightest bit of armor plating, and generally uncomfortable. In addition, once the Air Force decided to make the parachute a mandatory part of the FAC's flight equipment, there was even less room on the seat.

Parachutes were not liked. They made the already difficult problem of exiting the aircraft, which had a door only on the right side, more difficult. Still it must be acknowledged that the parachute did save some lives. One young FAC ran his O-2 into another O-2 while relieving his partner over a target area at nearly 13,000 feet above the ground. Thanks to his altitude, he had time to kick the left side window out and squeeze himself out of his uncontrollable aircraft. Miraculously he survived. Most pilots were rather skeptical about their own ability to carry out such an emergency procedure, however. The other technique was to unstrap, cross the cockpit, and exit via the right door—no small task in my opinion.

Handicapped by its civilian origins, the "Oscar Deuce" nevertheless has earned a niche in the ranks of illustrious combat aircraft. It served well above the jungles, swamps, and mountains of Vietnam and Laos; and courageous pilots did remarkable things with it.

CAPT. TIMOTHY KLINE flew F-4Cs for 4 years (1966–69) at RAF Woodbridge, U.K., and later served as forward air controller and air liaison officer to the Royal Thai Army at Bearcat, Republic of Vietnam. He is currently an instructor in history at the USAF Academy and flies the T-33 aircraft.

USN PHOTO

A Navy Bronco takes off from Vietnamese air base in 1969 to provide air cover for a river patrol boat in the Mekong Delta area.

The OV-10 Bronco with two rocket launchers mounted under its fuselage.

OV-10 Bronco

JAMES A. RICHMOND

LONG before I ever saw the OV-10 I had read several articles concerning its development as a triservice counterinsurgency aircraft; I had also seen artists' conceptions of the airplane as well as early pictures of it in *Aviation Week*. When I first actually saw the Bronco, on the ramp at McClellan Air Force Base during a stopover there while I was flying the C-141, it gave me the impression of being a prehistoric bird or a giant flying insect. The airplane sat high above the ramp on its spindly looking main gear, while its short wings and twin booms combined to give it the appearance of being ready to leap into the air. The oversize, unusual-shaped canopy was undoubtedly this thing's eye on the world. One approached the Bronco almost cautiously; unlike other forward air controller (FAC) aircraft, there was no doubt that the OV-10 was built to go to war, and its four sponson mounted machine guns gave it a certain air of authority.

Notification that it was my turn to go to Southeast Asia came soon after my first physical encounter with the OV-10, so with a favorable impression in my mind I asked for and was given the assignment to fly OV-10s during my tour of duty there. It was still another year before I was to fly the Bronco and fall in love with it. Training in the OV-10 and the fine art of being an FAC was conducted at Hurlburt Field, Florida. After a few hours of classroom instruction and study, a pilot was ready for his first flight. Right away the combination of the airplane and the mission stirred a "kick the tires, light the fires" image in me, and I quickly developed a habit of kicking the tires during the exterior inspection. There really wasn't that much to the exterior inspection anyway: the pilot had to check the level of the fuel in the drop tank, make sure the armament was installed properly, check the general condition of the aircraft, and—in Southeast Asia—make sure there were no bird nests in the exhaust stacks. He was then ready to get into the airplane.

After flying other ejection-seat aircraft that had required lugging an unwieldy parachute out to the aircraft and stowing it in the seat prior to getting in, it was a real pleasure to walk out to the OV-10 wearing only an ejection system harness. But there the pleasure stopped. Getting into the

USN PHOTO

Two Broncos fly low over Vietnam in search of enemy activity.

Bronco was almost impossible for the novice and never mastered gracefully by anyone. Perhaps North American planned it that way in order to get the pilot in the right frame of mind for the demanding mission. To enter the cockpit he unfolded a small step in the right side of the aircraft, mounted via the step, and climbed in through the right-side canopy, which folded upward like the gull-wing doors on a 1952 Mercedes 300SL coupe. After getting situated in the seat, the pilot then needed help attaching his shoulder harnesses, which were also his parachute risers. Attaching the shoulder harness solo wasn't impossible, but it required considerable contortions and took a lot of time.

Once in the cockpit he could get on with the business of getting the OV-10 airborne. The interior preflight was easy, followed a logical sequence, and could be completed in approximately one minute—providing the pilot didn't get hung up on cranking the rudder pedals in or out. Starting the engines was also easy; they had the smooth continuous windup that was typical of a turboprop. Since the OV-10 was intended for use at forward fields where ground power equipment might not be available, it was designed to start on its battery; but the Air Force soon found out that making routine battery starts on the Bronco was not really the way to go. A battery start was generally slower, was hard on the batteries and engines, and had to be accomplished without full engine instrumentation. The engines were started with the propellers "on the locks," which was in a flat pitch position. This required that the throttles be moved momentarily into the reverse range in order to get the props "off the locks" prior to taxiing.

Taxiing the OV-10 was easy but a little tricky, and it was an operation that was always closely scrutinized and invariably criticized by almost every instructor pilot. Turns could be accomplished by use of differential braking, differential power, the nosewheel steering system, or any combination of the three. Using differential braking was usually frowned upon unless it was necessary for a very tight turn; nosewheel steering was used only for turns requiring more turning power than was available from differential power; differential power was normally used for small turns and to keep the aircraft going straight. As can be seen, when to use which system was largely a judgment matter and easily open for instructor criticism.

Reaching the end of the runway, the OV-10 was almost ready for takeoff; but as with all aircraft with an external ordnance load, an end-of-the-runway inspection and weapons arming was required. In the daytime this was a quick operation; at night we had to shut down the engines, since an instance had occurred where an armorer had been seriously injured at night when he had accidentally moved into the invisible arc of the spinning propeller. After being armed and collecting the pins from the armorer, we were ready to go.

On the runway the power levers were advanced to the takeoff and land position, the throttles were advanced to 100% rpm, the engine instruments were given a quick check and we were under way. Originally designed as a short takeoff and landing (STOL) aircraft, the OV-10 could lift off at 73 knots in 700 feet on a standard day at sea level, clean, with full internal fuel. That was fairly impressive to most of us reading the Bronco flight manual for the first time. After all, most of us were transplanted transport, bomber, or fighter pilots used to much longer takeoff rolls and higher liftoff speeds. However, we were soon dismayed to find that the STOL liftoff was below the minimum safe single-engine speed and that at least one pilot had crashed after losing an engine on a STOL takeoff. We were, therefore, restricted to using a higher rotation speed—one that got us airborne after the minimum safe single-engine speed.

But we were in for yet another surprise, particularly those of us headed for Thailand. The fully loaded 300-gallon centerline fuel tank and its associated effects on takeoff performance gave extra drag and extra weight, increased liftoff speed, and lengthened takeoff roll; it also severely decreased climb performance. If an engine were lost immediately after takeoff, the airplane was too heavy to fly; it would be necessary to jettison the external stores or put the aircraft back on the runway. Despite all the problems the Bronco always seemed to get airborne with little difficulty. I don't recall ever aborting a takeoff for any serious problem. Low torque seemed to be the main cause of aborted takeoffs, but that was generally evident before the brakes were ever released.

Once in the air the OV-10 performed nicely with the training load we had at Hurlburt Field but more sluggishly with a full combat load in Southeast Asia. Nevertheless, for me and most of those I knew, flying the OV-10 was a welcome interlude between bomber, tanker, or transport assignments. Invariably the first things that impressed all pilots flying the Bronco were its turning performance and visibility. Old-timers would have said that it would turn on a dime and give you five cents change. I don't know about that, but the turning performance was spectacular and a particular plus for the FAC. He could stay over a target and observe the activity below very easily because of the turning performance and visibility. In the area of speed most pilots were not impressed, but there were few grumbles about its fairly slow top speed either. After reading the flight manual and seeing 350 knots as the top speed, I had sort of expected to be able to attain 350 knots easily. That was not the case. The Bronco was power limited and could attain only about 210 knots clean and 170 knots with a combat load at 5,000 feet. Many Broncos would not even do that. I tried to get the OV-10 up to 350 knots a couple of times but found that it was a difficult task, requiring a steep dive angle and full power.

Nearly all Air Force pilots like an aerobatic airplane, and the Bronco was fully aerobatic. The two booms with twin rudders gave the airplane plenty of directional control, and the exceptionally large elevator was effective well below stall speed. The ailerons were assisted by a set of spoilers on the top of each wing which combined to give the OV-10 a good roll rate at all airspeeds. The flight controls were so effective that the OV-10 could literally be flown out of a spin. The engines were the only big limitation on its aerobatic performance. After a few over-the-top maneuvers we would have to stop and climb to a good starting altitude again. In fact, when the airplane was heavy, a level 60° bank turn couldn't be maintained. Even with its problems, the Bronco was really a little fighter. There were those of us who occasionally couldn't resist the urge to try out some aerial combat on a willing friend, and then we saw just how maneuverable the OV-10 really was.

I have heard some pilots who flew the aircraft but never in combat say that the Air Force should not have bought the OV-10, but I doubt that these critics were considering the alternatives—the O-1 and the O-2. All the OV-10 pilots I knew in Southeast Asia thought the OV-10 did an excellent job. The superb visibility, short turn radius, relatively large ordnance load, and excellent loiter time (especially with the 300-gallon centerline drop tank) made the Bronco an unequaled FAC aircraft. The Navy and Marines also used it as a light attack aircraft.

The OV-10 could accept several different combat configurations on its five external stations. On the centerline station the Air Force birds usually carried a jettisonable fuel tank, and the four sponson stations carried the ordnance. The sponsons were two small winglike protuberances on the bottom of the fuselage that appeared to be an afterthought. The normal ordnance loads carried by FAC aircraft were pods of seven 2.75-inch folding fin smoke rockets for daylight target marking or canisters of flares or ground marks for night target marking. In addition to the external ordance the OV-10 carried four M-60 machine guns, two mounted in each sponson. The machine guns, however, were normally used only on special missions. Starlight scopes were mounted in some airplanes for night work, and in 1971 a few Broncos were modified to accept a laser illuminating device to guide the recently developed smart bombs to their targets.

The FAC's job was to perform visual reconnaissance, direct air strikes, and assess the damage after an air strike. In Vietnam where the plane could work as low as 1,500 feet above the ground, reconnaissance was performed with the naked eye; along the Ho Chi Minh trail where the plane was driven up to a minimum altitude of 6,500 feet above the ground by antiaircraft fire, the FAC had to perform reconnaissance with the aid of binoculars. The large expanse of Plexiglas in the OV-10 made this an easy job whether working with the unaided eye or binoculars. Initially, trying to watch the ground below with binoculars and fly the airplane as well was not easy, but after a while the pilot got used to doing both jobs at once.

USN PHOTO

A Navy Bronco fires a Zuni rocket at a target in the Mekong Delta.

Once a target was located and the fighter/bombers were ready to work, the FAC had to mark the target accurately and direct the strike. Marking a target with the OV-10 required arming a rocket pod, setting the desired depression in the bomb sight, rolling into a dive on the target, and firing a smoke rocket. Firing or dropping ordnance from an OV-10 could be accomplished only from the front seat, but instructor pilots prided themselves on being able to line up on a target from the rear seat and direct the pilot in the front seat to fire with greater accuracy than the pilot in the front seat could achieve by using the bomb sight. Marking a target at night with flares or ground marks was done from level flight with the help of a navigator FAC in the back seat. After an air strike was completed, the FAC assessed the damage to the target and reported it to the strike flight and the airborne controller.

Radio coordination was a big job for the FAC, since it required listening to two or three radios simultaneously. He was constantly requesting air strikes, directing air strikes, or making reports. The OV-10 was well equipped for this portion of the FAC's job but poorly designed. It had at least one of each type of radio used by the Air Force or Army; but switching from one radio to another, talking on the radio, and flying the airplane really required three hands. Somehow we managed, but never with the greatest of ease.

Range was of little importance to the FAC aircraft, but endurance was. With the 300-gallon drop tank the pilots thought that, if anything, the Bronco had too much endurance! Normal missions were four and a half to five hours long—an awfully long time to be sitting immobile, strapped into an airplane. We put down five and a half hours as the endurance on our mission sign-out sheets, but I once flew a five-and-three-quarters-hour mission and still returned to the base before reaching the prescribed minimum fuel state.

Returning from a mission the standard approach for an OV-10 was a 360° overhead pattern, and that was what the pilots liked best. However, at most bases we couldn't fly a 360° overhead pattern with any ordnance on board, and it was seldom that we returned without a few rockets left over from the day's mission. Therefore, our pattern usually had to be a large box pattern flown outside the base perimeter. At Nakhon Phanom most Bronco pilots liked to announce their return by making a high airspeed, steep bank turn onto the outside downwind leg of the traffic pattern, which was just opposite the quarters area and near the busiest section of the base. The doppler effect took care of the arrival announcement by sending the roar of the engines right into the quarters area. There was even a small competition, particularly among the lieutenants, to see who could arrive with the loudest roar. The controllable pitch of the propellers made a steep glide slope possible and spot landings easy. Once on the ground the combination of reverse thrust and wheel brakes gave the Bronco a short landing roll.

One of the ideas incorporated into the Bronco as a triservice counterinsurgency aircraft was its multimission capability. Provision had to be made for paratroops, but to the best of my knowledge troops never bailed out of the OV-10. That was something reserved exclusively for the pilot and extra crew member in the tandem seats. Fortunately the OV-10 had one of the best and most reliable ejection systems around. I am a particular fan of its ejection system because I had to use it on one occasion after my plane was hit by antiaircraft fire. The seat was rocket-launched right through the canopy of the aircraft. The ejection itself was rather soft by most standards. No one I knew who ejected from the OV-10 ever suffered any aftereffects more than a little soreness and some singed hair on the back of his calves from the rocket blast. The ejection sequence could be initiated at any speed or altitude within the envelope of the aircraft with an almost sure chance of success. One inexperienced back seater even punched out successfully while the aircraft was parked, when his arming pin streamer became tangled with the ejection D-ring and he initiated the ejection sequence accidentally. The seat worked just as advertised, and he walked away from his experience somewhat shaken by his sudden unplanned departure from the airplane but otherwise okay.

CAPT. JAMES RICHMOND'S flight and tactical training in the OV-10 was conducted at Hurlburt Field, Florida, in late 1969, after which he was assigned to the 23rd Tactical Air Support Squadron, Nakhon Phanom RTAFB, Thailand. He is presently assigned to the 4950th Test Wing, Wright-Patterson AFB, Ohio.

As in any flying organization, talking about our missions and the airplanes we flew occupied a great deal of our off-duty time. Using those discussions as an indicator of how the FAC pilots felt about the OV-10, I would say that there were few who didn't love the airplane. It wasn't fast, it wasn't very powerful, it wasn't aerodynamically beautiful, but it had a place all its own among Air Force aircraft.

P-38 Lightning

ROYAL D. FREY

CONFEDERATE AIR FORCE

A SOFT muffled sigh drifted across the Santa Ana Army Air Base preflight center. Rushing from my tent, I saw for the first time that intriguing and mysterious airplane about which I had so often read, the Lockheed P-38 Lightning. It not only looked different from any other airplane I had ever seen—it even sounded different. The preflight center was located only a couple of miles west of Santa Ana Army Airfield; at the time I reported as an aviation cadet for classification and preflight training (August 1942) a squadron of P-38s was based on the field. Nearly every day we cadets could see P-38s taking off and later buzzing the runway prior to landing. Even in my wildest dreams I never imagined I would ever be so fortunate as to fly one of them.

While I was at Basic Flying School at Pecos, Texas, in February 1943, the famous long-distance civilian pilot Jimmy Mattern brought in a P-38 for flight demonstration. Upon seeing him roll it off the deck into a dead engine, I was convinced that this was the plane for me. I ran across the ramp to my instructor and pleaded my case—the P-38 was what I really wanted to fly. The crocodile tears in my eyes must have turned the trick, for I was next sent to Williams Field near Phoenix—the AAF's twin-engine fighter school.

After getting 70 hours in the AT-17, 6 hours dual gunnery in the AT-6, and 10 hours in the AT-9 (if you can fly the AT-9 without getting killed, you can fly anything!), I was scheduled for checkout in the RP-322. The RP-322 was known as the "castrated P-38" because it lacked turbo-superchargers. It also lacked guns, armor plate, and standard P-38 communications equipment. It had evolved from the Lightnings originally purchased by the British and subsequently taken over by the AAF for training purposes.

Although the RP-322 lacked much of the P-38's equipment, it also lacked much of the P-38's weight. As a result, at full throttle on the deck it scooted like a scalded deer. However, at 15,000 feet it became a dud, not even able to hold its own against antiquated P-40s from Luke Field on the other side of Phoenix.

After getting 10 hours in the RP-322, I was awarded my wings on May 20, 1943, and sent to Operational Training Unit (OTU) at Muroc Army Air Base (now Edwards AFB). Here began the most exciting and carefree period of my life—my brief career as a P-38 pilot. It came to an abrupt end less than nine months later when I was forced to bail out over Germany.

With its tricycle gear, counterrotating props, and inherent stability the P-38 was extremely easy to fly. Once trimmed for straight and level flight, it was a hands-off airplane. If you put it into an unusual attitude (within reasonable limits) and then got off the controls, it would slowly waddle and oscillate around in the air and eventually return to straight and level flight. This was because its center of lift was above its center of gravity—i.e., most of the mass of the airplane was slung under a wing having a large amount of dihedral. Other fighters of the era with their low wings (and the consequential lower center of lift) tended to drop off on one wing or the other, since the center of lift would always tend to seek a position above the center of gravity. In the P-38 this feature was built in.

Another excellent feature built into the P-38 was its stall characteristic—it stalled from the center section outward to the tips. As a result, in a panic break with an enemy plane behind you, you could pull the P-38 into such a tight turn that it would begin to buffet, but you would still have remarkable aileron control.

One day in July 1943 while landing at Portland, Oregon, on my first cross-country in a P-38, I learned how completely forgiving was the Lightning. Flying No. 2 on the break, I got much too low on the final turn. The runway at Portland somehow completely disrupted my perspective. (I later learned it was covered with tar and wooden chips and was much wider than normal—to me at the time it appeared almost as wide as it was long.) In any case, there I was on the treetops off the approach end of the runway, needing to tighten my left turn in order to line up for landing, but much too low to steepen my bank without dragging my left wing tip through the top of someone's house. So I gradually began to feed in more and more left rudder. Suddenly, without any warning, the rudder pedals shook violently several times and then the left rudder pedal slammed my foot backward to the full rear position—a complete rudder stall. I immedi-

Lightnings of the 15th Air Force in formation over Yugoslavia in 1944.

ately poured on the throttles for a few seconds to increase my airspeed slightly, and the rudder pedals returned to neutral. I dumped full-flaps, chopped throttles, and still made a normal routine landing. My buddy flying No. 3 a short distance behind me never noticed anything unusual. Had we been in single-engine fighters, he would probably have seen my plane flip into the trees and explode.

With its inherent stability, counterrotating props, muffled engine exhausts through the turbos, and fairly heavy weight, the P-38 was a sheer delight on takeoff. You would take the runway, line up and brake to a full stop, and advance the throttles to at least 44 inches of manifold pressure to where the turbos would cut in. The nose would gradually drop as the increasing pull of the props forced the nose strut to compress, and the whole plane would shake and vibrate, waiting to be released from the bonds that held it. A quick glance across the instrument panel and off the brakes.

Up popped the nose and you bounded forward like a racehorse from the starting gate.

As you gathered speed down the runway, the heavy weight of the plane deadened any bumps, and you felt as if you were in a Cadillac. At the same time the turbo exhausts made the engines sound extremely muffled as if you were in a high-powered pleasure boat: no loud crackling or roar so usual in those days of reciprocating engines. No torque to swing the nose, and beautiful visibility down the runway from the level attitude of the tricycle gear. At 70 mph you gently eased back on the control yoke, and at 95–100 mph the plane lifted softly into the air. What complete comfort for a combat plane!

One of the greatest bugaboos of the P-38 was engine failure on takeoff. Consequently we had drilled into us critical single-engine speed on takeoff—130 mph. Even before God, Motherhood, and Country came that 130 mph as soon as possible after your wheels left the runway. As a result, as soon as the plane broke ground, you dropped your nose to maintain level flight 5–10 feet off the runway. You always added 10 mph for next-of-kin and another 10 mph or so as a fudge factor. Then you gradually lifted the nose for optimum climb speed of 160 mph. If in a populated area, the tendency was to hold the plane on the deck and build up as much speed as possible before beginning your climb—it was much more impressive to the taxpayer who might be driving his auto down a street off the end of the runway when your props cut through the air within a hair of his head. We all knew it was legalized buzzing but defended it fervently; we had to get that safe single-engine speed or die!

I do not personally recall anyone ever losing an engine or prop on takeoff. I do remember hearing of a few instances of a runaway prop, but many of them might have been caused by the pilot taking off with one of his Curtiss electric props locked in fixed pitch.

My only personal experience with this type of difficulty on takeoff resulted from an oil cap coming loose while taxiing along the rough grass runway at Wittering RAF Station in England. On liftoff I noticed oil pouring along the cowling of my right engine. I first hit the right feather switch and then trimmed in left rudder and left aileron after pulling the mixture control to idle-cutoff. I do not remember my exact airspeed as I crossed the boundary at the far end of the field, but I could not have been doing more than 135–140 mph. At this fairly low speed, the plane was anything but the snarling, uncontrollable monster I had been led to believe.

Landing the P-38 was as smooth and pleasant an operation as takeoff. We would dive onto the field, buzz the runway at about 10 feet, and peel up into a steep climbing turn. With no torque there was no necessity for constantly cranking in rudder trim, and the nose did not wander all over the sky as airspeed dropped off. While on top of the peel-up, in a vertical bank almost on our back, we chopped throttles and moved the flap handle into half-flap position (maneuver flaps). With no power and so much increased lift, plus the great stability of the plane, we could pull it around onto the final approach as tightly as was required in order to line up with the runway. In fact, we soon got to be such "hot pilots" that we would still be in a steep diving turn as we crossed the boundary of the field, as full flaps came down, rolling out just before the main wheels touched the ground.

The P-38 was an excellent gun platform, although it was more diffi-

The author's P-38J after it had been shot down in Nazi Germany in 1944.

cult than in a P-47 or P-51 to get strikes on a target because the four .50 caliber guns and 20 mm cannon were grouped so closely together in the nose. However, if we got any strikes at all, we had a much better chance of getting a victory; those five weapons put out such a heavy column of projectiles that they bored a large hole through anything they hit.

The P-38 had the famous Fowler flap, which, at half-extended position, greatly decreased turn radius at altitude at the expense of very little additional drag. This feature, incorporated in the P-38 for combat, was given the name "maneuver flaps." With maneuver flaps I actually turned with late-model Spitfires during "rat races" over England and turned inside FW-190s in action over Europe.

There was a poor design feature associated with the maneuver flaps, however—namely the control lever, located on the right side of the cockpit. Since the P-38 was flown with the left hand on the throttles and the right hand on the control wheel, any use of maneuver flaps required the pilot to keep his right hand dancing from the wheel to the lever while at the same time moving his left hand from the throttles to the wheel every time he took his right hand off the wheel to move the flap lever. Whoever gave the final approval for the location of the flap handle in the P-38 certainly must not have given any thought to its use in combat.

Although the P-38 could turn very tightly once it got into a bank, getting it into the bank was another matter. Late K series and L series Lightnings had aileron boost, but this feature came too late for those few of us who took on the Luftwaffe deep inside Germany in those grim days of late 1943 and early 1944. Because of the weight of the plane and the poor leverage of a control wheel compared to that of a control stick, the plane's roll rate approximated that of a pregnant whale. If we ever got behind a single-engine fighter in a tight turn, all the other pilot had to do was flip into an opposite turn and dive; by the time we had banked and turned after him, he was practically out of sight.

One day on a local flight over England I noticed that by jamming in quite a lot of rudder a second or two before trying to bank, I was apparently able to speed up the plane's roll response by lessening the force needed to turn the wheel. Whether it actually had any effect or not is a good question, but it did a lot for my mental attitude.

One trick I once used (other P-38 pilots may also have used it at times) when a German plane got close behind me in a tight left turn was to chop right throttle and kick full right rudder along with right aileron. I seemed to snap up and over to the right, and although I am certain I never approached a spin, I do not know to this day exactly what maneuver the plane executed. However, the German plane could not follow me through it, and that was the important factor. I never needed to try this trick in a right bank, but the resulting maneuver probably would have been the same though in the opposite direction.

The P-38 had a combat tactic that was very effective against German fighters but not taught to or known by many P-38 pilots. Luckily I was one of the exceptions. On January 4, 1944, the 8th Air Force bombed Kiel. That evening while reading the intelligence TWX (teletype printout) of the mission, I noticed a statement by a pilot of the 55th Fighter Group who reported that he had escaped from a German fighter by pouring on full throttle and going into a steep corkscrew climb to the right.

The next day the 8th went back to Kiel, and this time I went along on escort. My flight of four P-38s was bounced by twenty-five to thirty FW-190s of the yellow-nose variety from Abbeville. A string of six or more of them got in behind me before I noticed them, and just as No. 1 began to fire, I rolled into a right climbing turn and went to war emergency of 60 inches manifold pressure. As we went round and round in our corkscrew climb, I could see over my right shoulder the various FW-190 pilots booting right rudder attempting to control their torque at 150 mph and full throttle, but one by one they flipped over to the left and spun out. Incidentally, although I had been told in the States that it was not possible, I could actually see tracer bullets leave their barrels and zip toward me!

Upon landing back in England, I was told that my plane whistled as I circled for landing. There was good reason—the left wing outside the boom was shot so full of holes that it had to be replaced. Those FW-190 pilots had been able to get sufficient lead to hit my left wing, but none had been able to get that little extra bit of lead needed to knock out my left engine or put a burst of fire into the cockpit.

In addition to an agonizingly slow roll rate, the P-38s I flew in combat had two other very limiting features—restricted dive and cockpit temperature. It was suicide to put the P-38 into a near-vertical dive at high altitude; all we P-38 pilots knew it, and I believe all the Luftwaffe pilots knew it, for they usually used the vertical dive to escape from us. You could "split-S" and do other vertical-type maneuvers at high altitude; and as long as you continued to pull the nose through the vertical, you always held your airspeed within limits. But let the nose stay in the vertical position for more than a few seconds and you reached what was termed "compressibility" in those days. The nose would actually "tuck under" beyond the vertical position, and it would be impossible to recover the plane from its dive. The only salvation was to pop the canopy, release your seat belt, and hope you would clear the plane as you were sucked from the cockpit. The 20th Group lost two P-38s in vertical dives over England before we went operational, but both pilots bailed out successfully (although one of them almost killed himself when he popped his chute too soon).

According to a Lockheed tech rep who once visited us, theoretically the air was sufficiently dense at 1,500 feet *below* sea level for the P-38 to *begin* pulling out of a high-speed vertical dive. Such a statement did little

Cockpit of the P-38.

to bolster my confidence. Later Lightnings had dive brakes under the wings to correct this problem, but they were too late to be of value to me.

The other limiting feature, cockpit temperature, would be more correctly identified as "paralyzing." Cockpit heat from the engine manifolds was nonexistent. When you were at 30,000 feet on bomber escort and the air temperature was —55° F outside the cockpit, it was —55° F inside the cockpit. After 30 minutes or so at such a temperature, a pilot became so numb that he was too miserable to be of any real value; to make matters worse, he did not particularly care. Only his head and neck exposed to the direct rays of the sun retained any warmth.

Not only did the numbness seriously decrease a pilot's efficiency, but the bulky clothing he wore further restricted his efforts. For example, I wore double-thickness silk gloves, then heavy chamois gloves, and topped these with heavy leather gauntlets (all British issue). Inside all these layers were fingers almost frozen stiff and completely without feeling. Flipping a single electrical switch required deep concentration, skill, and luck, and the P-38 cockpit was loaded with electrical switches. How we envied the P-47 and P-51 pilots with a heat-producing engine in front of them to maintain a decent cockpit temperature.

The greatest problem of all with the P-38 over Europe in 1943–44 was its engines, or rather its engine installation. When the AAF decided to add more internal fuel to the P-38 and thereby increase its range, the only place more tankage could be placed was in the leading edges of the wings where the intercoolers were located. So leading edge tanks for about one hour's additional endurance were installed, and the intercooler radiators were moved to the lower noses of the booms under the prop spinners.

The intercoolers worked fine in this position, but the adjacent oil coolers were now much too efficient. We would put up a Group strength of 48 planes and if 30 got to the target, we considered ourselves fortunate. On every mission plane after plane would turn back for England once we had reached high altitude, primarily because of an engine that had blown up or a turbosupercharger that had "run away"—i.e., uncontrollable overspeeding.

A couple of months after my left engine had blown up while I was flying deep inside Germany (an event that led to my capture), Colonel Mark Hubbard, 20th Group CO, arrived at Stalag Luft I, my POW camp on the Baltic Sea north of Berlin. In a conversation one day he remarked that during the first three months the 20th Group was on operations, it had the equivalent of a complete turnover in pilots—70 percent of which could be attributed either directly or indirectly to engine trouble. What a needless waste of highly trained men to the enemy!

A Lockheed tech rep explained that at the tremendously low air temperatures in which we were flying, the oil in the radiators cooled to such an extent that its viscosity resembled that of molasses. It simply refused to flow sufficiently, and the engines would eventually explode or the oil-type turboregulators would malfunction.

The P-38 had a horrible reputation when it came to a pilot bailing out. The horizontal empennage, which we dubbed "the cheese knife," was considered a menace. In reality it was less of a threat than the stabilizers on the P-47 and P-51, simply because it was located farther to the rear from the P-38 cockpit, thereby providing more chance for a pilot to clear it on bailout. In addition the P-38 did not have a fin and rudder directly behind the cockpit which the pilot had to avoid. The only fighter pilot I knew in POW camp to strike the tail of his plane was a fellow who bailed out of a P-51D. When I was forced to bail out over Germany, I rolled my P-38 onto its back and dropped clear without any difficulty.

The experience that led to my capture in February 1944 sheds light on the performance of the P-38 in combat. Five Lightnings dove on four Me-410s and two Me-110s in a combat over Germany, and the Luftwaffe pilots scattered in all directions. I decided that if I were going to have to chase one of the German planes, I might as well be heading toward England, so I selected an Me-110 scooting westward on top of the cloud deck. Having had a right engine shot out by an Me-110 rear gunner over Frankfort two weeks previously, I had developed quite a healthy respect for any rear gunner. Therefore, I lined up behind the German plane and dropped into the cloud deck, holding a steady compass course. When I slowly pulled up from the cloud layer, the Me-110 was slightly above me at a range of less than 200 feet. I took careful aim at its belly through my gunsight and let it have all four .50 caliber guns and the 20 mm cannon. The Me-110 flamed so rapidly that the crew probably never had time to realize what had happened to them.

Quite elated, I pushed my prop pitches forward to 3,000 rpm and my throttles to 54 inches of manifold pressure, maximum allowable military power. Although the P-38 handbook allowed fifteen minutes of operation at military power, my left engine blew up after only three minutes. The Allison "time bomb" had once again held true to its reputation.

I feathered the left prop immediately and headed westward as before, hoping to reach England more than 300 miles away. However, the P-38J-10-LO had a design feature none of us pilots could ever quite fathom: it had only one generator, and it was on the left engine. (Later series J airplanes were produced with a generator on each engine.) Normally this would not have been a problem, but the cross-feed on the P-38 was electrical, and a pilot had to have electrical power to transfer his fuel from the tanks on one side of the plane to the engine on the other side. Even though I had turned off all electrical equipment immediately upon losing the left engine, I realized my cross-feed would probably drain my battery before my right engine had time to burn all the fuel in my two left tanks. I determined to stay on cross-feed until the battery went dead and then switch to my right tanks. This would probably never get me across the North Sea to England, but it should get me to Holland, where I had a chance of being picked up by the underground.

After flying on instruments for almost an hour, I broke through the western edge of the cloud layer into clear air; suddenly I saw five bursts of light flak walking in on me from the right side, exactly at my altitude. Then, to my utter horror, I heard the sixth one somewhere from below my plane. My mind flashed back to the bars in London in those days before I began flying ops when the bomber boys used to quip, "If you ever hear it, it's got you."

Their words were prophetic, for within a few seconds my right engine began smoking. To get away from the flak battery as rapidly as possible, I dove for the deck and leveled off on the treetops. I sped across forests and open fields with the smoke rapidly getting more intense. Before long I began to smell it as it seeped through the wing into the cockpit. It did not take much debate for me to decide I should not attempt to belly-land a smoking plane. Besides, the Germans, to the best of my knowledge, had not yet received a J series P-38 in any respectable condition worthy of close technical examination.

As I approached another forest, I decided to use the remaining "excess" speed from my dive for a zoom to sufficient height for bailout. As I reached the other side of the forest, I pulled up into a climb, leveled off, cranked in full-down nose trim, rolled the plane on its back, pulled the canopy release, and unlatched my safety belt. With flames now coming into the cockpit from around the right window, all these motions were performed almost as one, and I next felt myself drop into the rushing airstream.

Admittedly the P-38 was outperformed by the P-47 and P-51 in the skies over Europe, but many of its difficulties were the result of unnecessary design deficiencies and the slow pace of both the AAF and Lockheed in correcting them. One can only ponder about how much more rapidly the troubles would have been remedied if the slide-rule types had been flying the plane in combat against the Luftwaffe. But I will always remember the P-38 with the greatest fondness. Even with all her idiosyncracies, she was a real dream to fly.

LT. COL. ROYAL D. FREY is curator of the Air Force Museum, Wright-Patterson AFB, Ohio. During World War II he flew P-38s over Europe on long-range escort missions.

A P-39 Airacobra in flight.

P-39 Airacobra

RICHARD D. KENT

IT was in September 1942 at Napier Field in Alabama, while I was still a cadet flying T-6s, that I first saw the P-39. My desire was to be a fighter pilot (or pursuit pilot, as it was then termed), and watching this P-39 land and taxi up convinced me I'd made the right decision. It was beautiful—sleek, well armed, small—and the tricycle landing gear fascinated me since it was the first such gear I'd seen. In fact this was the first actual fighter I'd seen other than in pictures. The final reinforcement of my inclinations came when the P-39 took off, buzzed the field, and slow-rolled on the deck several times. Fortunately that deadly inhibitor now called "flying safety"—a fighter pilot really knowing his true flying abilities as well as his plane's idiosyncrasies—hadn't been permitted to dampen this P-39 pilot's spirit; the demands of the war took first priority.

My understanding is that the P-39 was designed and built prior to World War II to British specifications requiring a fast-climbing interceptor to destroy low-flying enemy bombers raiding England. The Airacobra was never used for that purpose for several reasons: the Germans attacked England with a different tactical approach, and the P-39 had a major flaw—extremely low fuel capacity—that severely limited its usefulness.

This aircraft was different in many ways from other contemporary fighters. Besides the revolutionary tricycle gear its in-line, air-cooled engine was located behind the cockpit. This feature permitted the use of a 37 mm cannon firing through the nose plus two .30 caliber machine guns firing through the prop and two .50 caliber machine guns in each wing. The pilot entered the aircraft from either of two doors similar to the two front doors of the modern automobile. To eject he could release either door, roll out of the seat, graze the wing, and fall under the tail. In a panic he could release both doors and literally be sucked out of the cockpit. A major disadvantage was that, if wounded or for some reason unable to use the emergency release on the doors, he couldn't roll the plane over and fall out as was possible in other fighters.

The P-39 handled well in the air: it was stable, an excellent gun platform, and very sensitive to the controls, as was the P-51. Quick and very minute corrections when in combat with an enemy aircraft, particularly the outstandingly maneuverable Japanese Zero, were definitely an advantage. The P-40 and P-47 were deficient in this aspect, since sheer strength was required to execute a high-speed turn or to recover from a high-angle, high-speed dive; a skillful but less strong pilot was at a definite disadvantage in these aircraft in these instances. Other advantages of the P-39 were its exceptionally high rate of climb from the ground to 12,000 feet (better than any other American fighter used in World War II) and its rapid acceleration and high rate of diving speed at any altitude.

However, its disadvantages outweighed the advantages by far. Upon climbing through 12,000 feet, you felt as if you had hit a brick wall. In combat, and given the chance, the climb from 12,000 feet to 25,000 or 35,000 was at a snail's pace. Because of the stubby wings, maneuverability above 12,000–15,000 feet was nil and not very good below that altitude. Your only hope was to lure the Zeros to a lower altitude or make one run at the enemy at altitude and dive for your life. Many times I approached the speed of sound in the P-39 with no trouble. If you had altitude, you could easily leave the Zero far behind, because the Zero's wings had a tendency to separate from its fuselage around 350 knots. However, by this time your fuel was critical and/or the enemy did overheads on you from their height advantage.

To briefly summarize, the P-39 was virtually worthless above 15,000 feet, and this was at a time when the enemy flew routinely at 35,000–45,000 feet. Fuel was a critical problem: air time in combat was at best 25–30 minutes, and we flew routinely over the ocean at Guadalcanal. Additionally, other than the standby compass we had no navigational equipment whatsoever. Fighting over water, out of sight of land, against better and more enemy aircraft in almost every instance, tended to make the P-39 pilot a restless individual to say the least. Many such pilots died because of lack of fuel to make it back to that tiny island or because they couldn't find the island. Returning at night with runway flare pots out because of enemy ground action or bombing from the air or sea further thinned our ranks. "Somebody up there liked us," however, for most of us from our original group of 13 pilots sent to Guadalcanal lived to tell war stories.

Certain taxiing, takeoff, and landing characteristics of the P-39 were excellent because of the tricycle gear. Runway width permitting, four-ship takeoffs and landings were routine. Taxi time and idle time on the ground, however, were critical, because the engines rapidly overheated. When flying with other aircraft (for example, P-40s, F-4Fs, P-38s), careful coordination with the other units was necessary; the short taxi time of the P-39s required that they take off either first or last. Because of the fuel limitations of the P-39, we generally took off last, to conserve fuel by eliminating the "form up" time lost when performing a coordinated mission or escorting bombers.

By far the most dangerous time was during the landing phase. Because of the short, stubby wings the stall symptoms normally encountered in other fighters rarely appeared in the P-39; many pilots were killed as a result of allowing their airspeed to become too low in the landing pattern. The very little if any advance warning of a stall provided too little time for the pilot to recover airspeed at the low level of the traffic pattern.

Another deadly factor was also due to the short wings and resultant airflow. When performing aerobatics at altitude or in ship-to-ship combat that resulted in an uncoordinated turn or too tight a turn, the plane was said to stall without warning and tumble end over end. Several pilots have told me this happened to them and it took 15,000 feet to recover. This tumbling characteristic was debatable—it never happened to me and, intentionally and unintentionally, I stalled the plane in almost every conceivable situation but at high enough altitude to recover. Perhaps I was just lucky to stall it in such a way as to avoid the tumble. These stalling factors, however, caused many pilots to avoid flying the P-39 whenever possible and contributed to its reputation as a dangerous plane to fly.

The short taxi time of the P-39 due to overheating resulted in the death of one of the finest pilots I ever knew. He had just shot down his fifth Zero a few days before. On a predawn takeoff the P-39s were lined up at one end of the field waiting for four P-38 flights to take off. The P-38s were taking off from the opposite end of the runway, but wind was not a factor to any great degree in the tropics, and the P-39s were planning to avoid the long taxi to the other end. Because of the heat, the P-39 pilots were sitting on their planes' wings watching the P-38s take off. The thirteenth P-38 either lost an engine or became spatially disoriented on the instrument takeoff, rolled over in the air shortly after liftoff, and crashed into the waiting P-39s.

Our combat formation was conventional—four aircraft in widespread, finger-tip formation with the two elements far apart to permit each element to turn inside the other in case of a rear attack on either element. This was adapted from the advice given us from such great pilots as Joe Foss, flying there before our arrival, who incidentally had a much better fighter in the F-4F (Wildcat) than we did in the P-39. We also flew a combat formation called the "squirrel cage." Unlike the Flying Tigers, we often escorted troopships and had to remain in their locale—we couldn't hit and run. When the top P-39 flight above 15,000 feet was forced by overhead attacks to dive, it was replaced by another flight that had time and fuel to climb above the current engagement and dive on the enemy. Meanwhile, the lowest flight immediately began climbing for height advantage again—hence the "squirrel cage." This rarely worked, because the combat was moving rapidly away by the time the slow-climbing P-39s were able to reach altitude again. However, as was true in World War I and in Korea and Vietnam, aerial combat rapidly lost the initial engagement altitude. The only situation in which the P-39 had a chance against the Zero was at 12,000 feet or below. Two of my victories were scored with the spray of the waves on my windshield partially obscuring my vision. I have seen both American and Japanese fighters clip the water in a tight turn and destroy themselves.

Now a few comments on my personal combat preferences. In aerial combat I never used the cannon, because its trajectory was much different from that of the six machine guns. I used the cannon while strafing ships or enemy land positions. It was highly effective against Japanese landing craft. One well-aimed cannon shot would not sink the landing craft but would clear the craft of soldiers because of the landing craft construction—a welded, round-bottom job similar to a bathtub. The ricochet effect of the cannon was devastating. In aerial combat I used only half the machine guns at one time to save ammo for the flight home; sometimes we had to fight 150 miles or more to get back, and woe to the pilot who didn't keep a reserve for that eventuality. Knowing the torque of the Zero engines, I anticipated the enemy to break up and to the right whenever I succeeded in getting on his tail. That gave me the fraction of a lead angle I needed to try to hit him. Because of the Zero's climb and turn ability, we got only one crack at him when he was aware we were behind him. If the Zero pilot dived with a P-39 behind him, he was a dead man; that was the one advantage we had, and most of the Japanese knew it. Some Japanese pilots were excellent flyers, and these were naturally the flight leaders. We would many times let the less capable wingmen get away just to try to down the leader. If we got him and had the fuel and ammo, the remainder were much easier pickings. However, I believe I'm safe in saying that most fighter pilots shot down by another aircraft never knew the enemy was near him until too late, if he knew at all.

I practiced gunnery every chance I had, because I felt that capability alone against the Zero helped reduce—not even—the odds a little in my favor. All we got against a Zero pilot who was aware we were in the area was a split-second, angle-off snap shot. If we missed, he would "get away to fight another day." I wanted that saying to apply to me, not the enemy.

Constant flying over the water made every pilot aware of his plane's crash-landing characteristics both on water and land. The P-39 was excellent in both instances because of its design; its fuselage was basically that used for the first jet aircraft of U.S. design. The convex belly of the P-39 enabled it to crash-land on the water with little shock to the pilot. Depending on speed, it skipped several times like a flat rock scaled on the water. That was the moment to roll out the door, for after several skips it dove straight for the bottom.

Our airstrip was parallel to the beach. One afternoon several of us were lying on the beach drying our flight suits after swimming in them (that was our way of doing our laundry) and watching several P-39 flights taking off on a mission. The engine of one of the P-39s quit as the pilot turned out to sea at about 500 feet. We watched him belly-land in the water about 50 feet offshore, roll out as the aircraft sank, and swim to shore directly in front of us. As he walked past on the way to the strip he remarked, "Thanks for your help, fellows. I hope I didn't disturb you." The only other remark was made by one of us: "You're welcome, Charlie, but don't come too close—you might drip on us." It was about three days before Charlie would speak to us again.

Early in the war, pilot experience upon arriving in the combat zone was extremely limited. My group had only 30 hours each in the P-39 and only two or three gunnery missions. Rear-area training was given when possible, but at that time this luxury was seldom attainable since the demand for combat pilots was too great or spare planes were too few. During lulls in activity a unique practice gunnery system was used. One plane flew in a varied and weaving pattern over a reef. A gunnery pattern was established with the pilots diving and firing at the aircraft shadow over the reef. It was dangerous, because some pilots in their target fixation dove into the reef; however, it was an invaluable aid in learning gunnery. That was how I determined the P-39 cannon could not be used in conjunction with the machine guns—its trajectory was too different and required an entirely different firing technique. From this gunnery practice and several subsequent aerial engagements, I also eliminated tracers in my guns. I felt that if I missed a Zero on the first squeeze, I wouldn't get a chance for another.

Tracers just helped him get advance warning that he might be in deep trouble.

The finest angle-off shot and kill I ever witnessed occurred one afternoon as we were returning from a mission. Several flights of P-40s on a CAP over Guadalcanal were engaged by Zeros. One P-40 pilot at about 2,000 feet had a Zero on his tail and couldn't shake him. Our flight was letting down for landing and, as usual, had no fuel for a second pass at the strip. We were in widespread formation and had a clear view of the P-40 and the Zero below us and flying 90° to us. My No. 4 P-39 (who was the closest to the two) made a sharp bank, fired at about a 70° angle-off at the Zero who was less than a ship's length behind the P-40, and blew him up. Without changing course we proceeded straight for the field and landed. That night the happy P-40 pilot gave us some Australian beer he'd "borrowed" from some Seabees or Marines in the area and had hidden for a special occasion.

Many other tales could be told beyond the dry facts known to all fighter pilots; as such personal tales are published, they will provide important knowledge for future generations about the sometimes incredible events that took place during a very bleak period of World War II.

LT. COL. RICHARD D. KENT flew the P-39 at Guadalcanal, the F-86 in Korea, and the C-7 in Vietnam. He retired in 1973.

Spitfire VIII

WHICH was the best Allied fighter of World War II? What's your favorite? If you spell it "favourite," it has to be the Spitfire—no doubt about it. But if you're American, particularly an American fighter pilot, you'll probably be one of a clique of supporters of the P-51, the P-47, the P-38, or possibly some Navy fighter. There are other candidates, but their supporters lean on emotion rather than logic.

The Spitfire was the Allied symbol of victory in the Battle of Britain, but it was relatively low in power, service ceiling, and firepower in those critical days of 1940. It had already been tested in the United States before we entered the war but didn't create any sensation. Its speed was only average—368 mph at 19,000 feet—and its service ceiling was only about

vs P-51 Mustang

CHARLES M. McCORKLE

33,000 feet with a combat load. What the Spit had going for it was its margin of superb maneuverability, and that seems to be what accounted for its earlier successes. Its great disadvantage lay in its meager fuel supply—sufficient for battling within a hundred or so miles from home but far short of U.S. standards. The Spit carried only 85 Imperial gallons (106 U.S. gallons) internally—far less than contemporary American fighters.

Long range and endurance weren't serious needs for Europe in late 1941, but they soon would be. When our B-17s first arrived in England and Eighth Air Force leaders were planning daylight bombing of Germany, U.S. commanders asked for RAF fighter escort as deep as possible—even all the way to Berlin. The RAF answer was, "But our fighters haven't the range." So Wright Field's Engineering Division was given the job: "Build enough range into the Spitfire so it can fly to Berlin and back to England."

When in 1940 North American offered the XP-51 to Wright Field, it was a good airplane but not yet great. It was flown and liked by the pilots of the Pursuit Project Office. It was not only faster than the others—particularly at a low altitude—but maneuverable and had plenty of range. Its test reports were forwarded to headquarters with favorable comments. Headquarters' reply stated that there was no requirement for an additional fighter; Bell, Curtiss, Lockheed, and Republic as well as Navy contractors were all building fighters. Also, we couldn't afford to dilute North American's B-25 effort. The British took on the XP-51 as a low-altitude fighter and photoreconnaissance aircraft because of their serious need for almost any quality aircraft and also because they discerned its talents.

Was it better than the Spitfire at this stage? The British never would have agreed that it was, although it was somewhat faster and had far greater range. The Spit could outturn and outclimb it and thus could defeat it in conventional dogfighting combat. Both airplanes were plagued by low horsepower at high altitude and had lower service ceilings than the Me-109s, which were still diving on the RAF at will. It should be pointed out in comparing these fighters that when the prototype Spitfire flew in 1936, it was an extension of several years' development, while the Mustang wasn't conceived until 1940. Thus in many ways they were of different generations, if we consider the acceleration of technical developments during wartime.

In 1942 came the achievement that brought both the Spit and the P-51 into the truly superior fighter category. This was the Merlin 61, an advanced Rolls-Royce engine with the new big second-stage blower. It was rated at 1,650 horsepower for takeoff; its high blower cut in automatically at about 20,000 feet, providing good performance on through the 30,000s and service ceilings in the 40,000s, outperforming all German engines in the upper regimes.

Spitfire squadrons began looking downward at any Germans they could find, and those became scarcer by the day as Spit VIIIs and IXs took to the air in 1943. Since Vs were not too distinguishable from VIIIs and IXs except at fairly close range, any formation of Spitfires had to be taken very seriously.

The P-51, meanwhile, was popular with RAF pilots. But its performance restricted it to low-altitude work, its additional weight making it inferior to the Spitfire V and many others at altitudes over 20,000 feet. Through the cooperation of its British ties, North American Aviation arranged to get two of the new Merlins to Wright Field for installation in two P-51s. North American agreed to pay for the modifications and the flight test work to be done. A mock-up board met and gave its recommendations, and work began on the new airplanes—the XP-51Bs. In late 1942 they were completed and testing began, closely monitored by Washington. A series of speed points was flown, and the top speed of the P-51B peaked out at 442 mph at 24,000 feet, a full 50 mph higher than that of the Allison-powered P-51A. The vastly improved ceiling of the aircraft also was apparent. When the magic number 442 was cabled to Washington in code, North American received an immediate order for 400 airplanes.

In the spring of 1943 the 54th Fighter Group, recalled with its P-39s from the Aleutians, was moved to Bartow, Florida, and reequipped with P-51A Mustangs. We became the first P-51 group in the States and were assigned to the 3rd Air Force as an RTU to train replacement fighter pilots. The Mustang was a delight to fly. It was a pilot's airplane—comfortable and

P-51s ready to take off from their base in Southern Italy, 1943.

Spitfire Mark IX equipped with wing tanks.

relatively roomy, everything where it was needed, plenty of speed and range, and (to the gratification of former P-39 pilots) a cockpit heater that worked. It had a "laminarflow wing" which reduced drag and allowed the modest Allison horsepower to zip us along at airspeeds we'd hardly ever seen. It was delightful, tractable, easy to fly; and our accident rate was quite low.

In the summer of 1943, I joined the stream of graduate replacement fighter pilots going overseas. Arriving in Sicily via Trinidad, Natal, Dakar,

Marrakech, and Tunis, I was assigned to the 31st Fighter Group, now stationed at Termine. And of all aircraft to have as its equipment—Spitfires! It had mostly Vs but was beginning to receive IXs and a few VIIIs, these latter with the pointed wings for high-altitude performance. The IXs looked like Vs should, but the Vs were equipped with large, ugly Vokes chin filters, and looked very dowdy compared to the glamorous machines that had defended Britain. But there they were—the world's best fighters, or so some claimed. I had some doubts but felt highly honored to be given command of the 31st and privileged to try out the Spitfire.

The 31st was preparing for the invasion of Italy, including the landing on the Salerno beaches of the ground elements of one squadron, so I had the opportunity of training in the Spit and worked from the rear ranks forward. Leaving the IXs to the experienced Spit pilots, who could use them to greatest advantage, I started in the Vs. The Spitfire V was no dream fighter, I discovered. It was light, delicate, easy to fly (a P-26–P-40 combination?) but showed little performance other than beautiful handling and very high maneuverability. The wing loading was about 28 pounds per square foot, compared to about 50 for the P-38s and P-40s and 40 or so for the P-51s. This gave the Vs unbounded maneuverability—the kind the

Left (above) and right (opposite) sides of a Mustang cockpit.

United States no longer produced because it was provided at the expense of speed and range. Although the Spitfire V is claimed to have had a top speed of 369 mph, those we had—equipped for the desert—were much slower. The 31st had been fighting superior-performance Luftwaffe fighters with them, and its record over the previous year was good but not impressive. They were truly a delight to fly, however, and great for aerobatics.

By now each squadron had several of the newer aircraft, and replacements of VIIIs and IXs trickled in slowly but steadily. While almost as maneuverable, they had greatly improved performance. They were powerful—they seemed to leap from our dirt runways and had starting rates of climb of nearly 6,000 feet per minute. The Spit IX reached 43,000 feet faster than had the P-51, but it really didn't want to climb much higher.

Despite the beautiful performance of these airplanes, their short range was a real headache to us. They carried internally (the V and IX) 85 Imperial gallons, equal to about 106 U.S. gallons. We carried for day-to-day missions an external blister tank of 30 Imperial gallons (37 U.S. gallons) for a total of 143 gallons. At consumptions of 60 gallons per hour and more, this was an appallingly small supply of fuel. It permitted a sweep of 200 miles or more in radius but for covering a beachhead from Sicily allowed us only a few minutes on station. So larger tanks were provided (blister tanks of somewhere near 60 Imperial gallons) so that two-and-a-half-hour missions were feasible, of which a full hour could be on patrol over the beachhead. (Such missions had become customary in the Mediterranean,

where beachhead patrol was flown over the beaches of Sicily, then Salerno, Anzio, and so on. Any air action of consequence necessarily converged on the landing beaches, so these were more than just routine missions.)

Even so, the range and duration of the Spit was sadly lacking. One means of making up this deficiency was to station the Spits as near to the front lines as possible. Of course that provided poor living conditions, even with our tents, but the excitement of occasional strafings kept everyone interested. No Spit mechanic had to be told to dig a slit trench beside his sleeping area—he usually dug it before he pitched his tent. Up there within sight and sound (and sometimes range) of the cannon fire you felt you were part of the war. As late as early 1944 we lost numbers of Spitfires to cannon fire—a dozen or so at Nettuno on the Anzio beachhead—a direct result of trying to station the aircraft as near as possible to the action.

The fall and winter of 1943, once the Salerno invasion was concluded, provided dull air action for Italy-based Spits. Now equipped almost entirely with VIIIs and IXs, the 31st had trouble finding a fight. Battle area patrol became usual; occasional sweeps were permitted, and some escort missions with B-25s or A-20s which never were molested from the air. Their direct opposition consisted of FW-190As as either fighters or dive-bombers, protected by Me-109Gs. Victories for Spits were steady but far from numerous. The Luftwaffe tactical air force played its game cautiously and well, considering that it was heavily outnumbered. It chose odd times for hit-and-run dive-bombing attacks in the battle area and struck with little warning; any lucky defenders who were in position to pursue were likely to be confronted by Messerschmitts following through at a higher altitude. Yet the 31st victory-to-loss ratio moved near 3 to 1—far better than its record with Spitfire Vs.

With late winter came Anzio, plenty of action, and a flurry of victories, along with orders to move to the Fifteenth Air Force and be re-equipped with P-51s. The P-51B already had been introduced into England in the Eighth Air Force, where it was serving as escort fighter. This was to be the role of the 31st in the Fifteenth Air Force. The first two P-51s soon were reported available at Oran in Algiers and were ferried to Italy where the 31st was still located at Castel Volturno, on the beach north of Naples, with one squadron on the Anzio beachhead at Nettuno.

Now we could see which was the better aircraft. Needless to say, the subject had received plenty of attention since the conversion had been announced. During a year-and-a-half of Spit operations both the pilots and the ground crewmen had become extremely partial to the Spitfire. Now came this new bird with great recommendations, but the 31st had believed and proved that the Spit could lick anything it encountered. Although a few weeks of flying a new aircraft nearly always makes it popular, here was a case where a test had to come first. After several pilots had become familiar with it, a Mustang and a Spit took off for scheduled "combat," flown by two top young flight commanders. Their approximate takeoff statistics were: Spit IX—horsepower 1,650, wing area 242, weight (optional) 7,300, wing loading 30; P-51B—horsepower 1,650, wing area 233, weight (optional) 10,000 (near), wing loading 43.

When the fighters returned, the pilots had to agree that the Spitfire had won the joust. The Spit could easily outclimb, outaccelerate, and outmaneuver its opponent; the P-51 could outdive and outrun the Spit. That sounds like faint praise for the P-51, but we must remember that our opponents were not Spits but Me-109s and that the P-51's climb and maneuverability actually were quite good—nearly as good as the Spit's. More important, the fuel capacity of the P-51 was so superior to the Spit's that an entirely different dimension was added to the combat capability comparison range. Range didn't come into play in this particular encounter, though its integration in the P-51 made the aircraft relatively heavy compared with the Spitfire, which thus had better maneuverability and climb. However, it could and did assure the emergence of the P-51 as the best of a new breed—the direly needed long-range escort fighter.

The former Spit leaders now had to plan a different mode of combat, based on these differences. More Mustangs came, and the 31st and other groups received them as they moved to the Fifteenth Air Force—the strategic arm of the Mediterranean Allied Air Forces. After a short period of re-equipping and training the P-51s were ready to go. The mission was different, the environment changed radically, and even the enemy—still the German Me-109s and FW-190s—changed.

Instead of the one- or two-hour sorties in the Spits, missions became five, six, and seven hours long—tied to the bomber stream of the Fifteenth, with one fighter group protecting each bomber wing. It was difficult to do this job well—a bomber wing usually stretched for many miles—but that's where the action was. The same pilots who had been unable to find a fight in the tactical war now were sometimes returning out of ammunition. In a fighter group results weren't assessed by survival or losses or munitions expended; they were assessed by victories and, to a degree, by victories versus losses. In both these measures this particular group excelled and went on to become the highest-scoring fighter group in the Mediterranean Theater.

MAJ. GEN. CHARLES M. MC CORKLE is one of the few pilots who flew both Spitfires and Mustangs; in fact he became an ace in both. Now retired, he is serving as a consultant for Fairchild Industries in Hawaii.

The incorporation of long range into the P-51 gave U.S. forces a fighter escort without peer. It could transport offensive forces so far that most of the enemy defensive units with their limited range could not join the fight that unlimited numbers of U.S. bombers and fighters had brought to a place of our choosing. This example of concentration at maximum range to attack enemy units piecemeal has the ring of classic military history studies.

How did the demands of war affect our fighters? The P-39, an interceptor by design, became a tank-buster. The P-47, a great high-altitude fighter and our strategic escort star, lost its role to the 51 and became a great fighter-bomber. And the P-51, which started as a low-altitude fighter, got the starring role of all. The Spitfire kept its missions the same throughout.

The answer to the basic question of which was the number one fighter of World War II: the Spitfire was best for the interceptor mission, while the P-51 was best for its work as an escort fighter, and each was a real pleasure to fly.

Note: This chapter was excerpted from an article in the December 1973 *Aerospace Historian*, © 1973 by the Air Force Historical Foundation.

XR-12 Rainbow

L. L. BRABHAM

IT was due to no lack of perfection in design but solely to the condition of the economy at the time that the Republic XR-12 was not placed in volume production and only the original order for two aircraft was completed. It is doubtful if any aircraft design has ever had such impact on the aviation community as did the Rainbow. It was the long-awaited solution to the problem facing the photoreconnaissance people and was heralded by airline officials as the ultimate answer to air transportation.

The aircraft was flown for the first time early in 1946, and I had the pleasure of demonstrating it in flight to heads of the world's leading airlines and their engineering pilots. Two of the airlines placed firm orders for the airplane and others placed options, but because of the uncertainty of postwar travel volume predictions one of the major orders was canceled, and this required termination of the other orders. The military was experiencing similar budgetary problems, and after firm orders were placed and then canceled several times the construction program came to an end, when the first airline fuselage was within one month of coming out of the jig. Just imagine, an airliner cruising at 450 mph in 1947! Probably the world's greatest expert in aerial reconnaissance and then head of the photo lab at Wright Field, General George Goddard, said when the program was terminated, "We have hung black crepe on all the doors of the photo lab."

World War II pointed up the paramount importance of aerial intelligence gathering; with the very best efforts of the photorecon units there was never enough photo coverage of potential targets and bomb damage to furnish even the minimum requirements of the commanders in the field. Up to this time the only photo aircraft were fighters or bombers that had been modified to accommodate cameras. From lessons learned the hard way, the Army Air Corps leaders laid out detailed requirements for what was to be the first photorecon aircraft embodying all the capabilities then thought to be necessary: (1) range of 4,000 statute miles; (2) cruise altitude of 40,000 feet; (3) cruise speed of 400 mph; (4) capacity for carrying a very large variety of photorecon equipment, including a 108-inch focal length camera then under development; (5) ability to process film in flight

The author awaits the all-clear signal to take the long-secret photorecon plane aloft on its first flight.

REPUBLIC AVIATION

The XR-12 Rainbow on its first official flight.

to save time after landing (in this regard we were working on radio transmission of data which would permit analysis by ground commanders before return of the photo mission).

The aircraft that seemed to meet all the requirements—the Rainbow —came out like this: weight 137,000 pounds; span 129 feet, 2 inches; length 98 feet, 9 inches; powered by four Pratt & Whitney R4360 Wasp Majors, each boosted by two large turbosuperchargers. The ideal power plant installation was a very ingenious design and deserves special comment. The engines were very tightly cowled, and air was forced to the front of each engine by a two-speed fan. To control the pressure drop a flush sliding ring was placed at the rear of the engine; the exit area thereby determined the drop in pressure over the engine. Thus the air at the front of the engine was compressed, the heat from the engine was picked up and spouted out the rear, and the result was a thrust gain rather than the usual cooling drag. The air for engine power, oil coolers, and intercoolers was ingested through openings in the leading edge of the wing between No. 1 and No. 2 engines and No. 3 and No. 4 engines. This saved much drag over projecting scoops and radiators.

Another bonus gained from the engine installation came from the unique positioning of the turbosuperchargers. The engine nacelles were quite long and extended well behind the main wing. The two turbos for each engine were installed in a reclining position in the rear of the nacelle with the discharge pointing rearward. The aft end of the nacelle made an ideal jet nozzle, and when the area was dimensionally correct we were provided with the equivalent of about 200 hp per engine in jet thrust—just about for free!

Familiarization with a project such as this presents no problem, since the crew has months or even years to follow engineering data as it is compiled, with results of wind tunnel tests and so on. By the time the first airplane is on the flight line, one's impressions are well formed; it is helpful if those of the flight crew are enthusiastic—as mine were. It is like a close relationship with an old friend which becomes even closer when you go for a ride in the air together.

For the first flight of the Rainbow I selected Oscar P. Hass as copilot and James J. Creamer as flight engineer. It might be interesting to note that Jim Creamer was a nineteen-year-old usher at Radio City Music Hall just six years before being a flight engineer. At the time of our XR-12 flight he was one of the most skilled aircraftsmen I have known.

After the Rainbow had been in preflight for a short time we were asked for a flight schedule and were able to give a tentative one. It was quite a surprise to read in the company newspaper a few days later that the entire plant would be given time off on that tentative date to see the first flight ever of the Rainbow. And at 10 o'clock sharp! In spite of everything that day arrived with several unsolved mechanical problems; but the excellent training of the ground crews paid off, and with the entire factory watching we taxied out for takeoff at exactly 10 o'clock.

The first takeoff of the Rainbow was easy and smooth, with those 16,000 horses really hurling the lightly loaded airplane into the air. It was obvious that the acceleration was such that gear speed of about 250 mph would be exceeded before the gear was up, so the aircraft was pulled up into a pretty steep climb until the gear was up and locked. The flaps were about half down for takeoff, and when we attempted to raise them there was no response. We decided to try to get as much out of the flight as possible so checked control responses and approaches to stalls and the usual things; then we attempted to get the airplane into landing configuration with gear down and full flaps. When the flap switch was placed in the down position, there was no action from the flaps, but the cabin did fill with dense smoke. About then we felt it was time to get this thing back on the ground, which we did without further delay. With half flaps and light weight I think I made my best landing on that first attempt. We soon learned what our problem had been: the two electric motors activating the flaps had burned up. After replacement we had no more flap trouble.

The best way an old fighter pilot might explain what it is like to

These two photos show open and closed positions of the ring that regulated the pressure drop over the engine.

REPUBLIC AVIATION

fly the Rainbow is to suggest that one take all the best flying fighters and lump the best of the best into one: there you have the Rainbow. This does not mean that there were no bugs; there were, and our job was to eliminate them.

Since the flying done on the XR-12 was totally of an experimental nature, it is a little difficult to follow the same descriptive format as for an established production aircraft. All flights were to obtain certain test information—best rate of climb and time to climb; and speed, power, and performance at all altitudes. Changes were made which resulted in better handling qualities; the result was an aircraft that had a well-balanced control force gradient, adequate response, and stability about all axes. Test data showed that best climb, glide, and landing speeds were in the conventional range for aircraft with comparable wing loadings.

During the flight test program a number of novel schemes were employed to get as much data per flight as possible. During the stability tests we placed a large tank in the front of the aircraft and one of equal size in the rear, connected by pipes and a water pump. We filled one tank with water and in flight could study longitudinal stability throughout the range of center of gravity by pumping the water in the quantities required for whatever CG was desired.

Engine and propeller deicing could be checked by a system for spraying water into the front of the engine; icing condition could be created by seeking a flight level where the desired temperature prevailed.

There was early concern that the extended Plexiglas nose would create visibility problems in rain and glare. To study these effects we mounted a nose section mock-up high on a truck; the crew and I spent a great deal of time on rainy nights chasing up and down runways under various types of lights, testing internal as well as external light effects. This proved valuable in pinpointing trouble areas before they came as a surprise under actual flight conditions.

One problem we were aware of was that the entry to the crew quarters was through a door in the rear. From there we had to detour around camera stations and various test installations to get forward. This was of some concern, since egress in an emergency might be difficult—although an Air Corps crew did successfully abandon one of the aircraft sometime later in the vicinity of Eglin Air Force Base, Florida.

The R-4360 Wasp Major engines were reliable and very easy to start. With external power plugged into the aircraft we usually started No. 2 engine first, then No. 1, followed by No. 3 and No. 4. This is standard practice for four-engine aircraft and gives some protection to ground crews. Because of false fire warnings we had to shut down and feather engines a number of times on takeoff. Since the engines were placed so far out on the wing, an outboard engine caused considerable but not objectionable yaw. Flight could be continued on any three engines from any point on the takeoff run on a 5,000-foot runway. Loss of either No. 2 or No. 3 engine was hardly noticeable.

On the early flights it was determined that the double-slotted flaps produced a great deal of drag at maximum deflection, and also that at less deflection the lift was not affected noticeably and the drag was greatly reduced; so we reduced the max flap down setting from about 55° to about 45°. At the 45° setting the approach and flare were very comfortable, and excessive power was not required to recover any loss of speed during approach.

Touchdown was smooth, and the adequate landing struts made the entire landing very soft. Aerodynamic calculations indicated a high stick force during the landing due to ground effect, but it was decided that the first flight would be made and the ground effect investigated. The stick force buildup during flare and touchdown was negligible; but if the stick force was monitored continuously, the ground effect did become pronounced as speed was reduced. I have compared this observation with pilots of many different types of aircraft, and there is no question that there is this brief but rapid buildup of stick forces due to ground effect during the deceleration phase of landing. I have personally checked this out in the DC-4 and the B-29 as well as in the Rainbow.

As for control forces, they were adequate for the aircraft. An aircraft of this size has very long distances from control wheel to control surface, and there is a problem in reducing friction and drag around pulleys. This problem was met satisfactorily in the XR-12, and the final configuration was very satisfactory. Later large aircraft had controls that were hydraulically boosted, and any desired feel could be built in.

The XR-12 had one of the early propeller-reversing systems installed as a backup for an experimental magnesium casted brake system. This reversible feature saved the aircraft in a landing at Mitchell Field when the brake castings burst and brakes were lost completely.

The Rainbow had a complete flight engineer panel, and the instruments at the pilot crew stations were kept to a minimum. I developed a system whereby the engineer was used to the fullest possible extent. Most taxi operations were powered by the engineer, who was an indispensable crew member on this aircraft.

Because the Rainbow was so easy to fly, one felt perfectly at home with it after only four or five hours and a couple of landings. I had done the prototype tests of the P-47 Thunderbolt and remembered the early phenomenon of so-called freezing stick at high Mach number. One day we were doing some kind of test in the XR-12 that required stabilizing in level flight with METO (maximum except takeoff) power at 35,000 feet. When the test was almost complete I asked the copilot if he noticed something radically wrong. He checked his panel and consulted with the engineer, then informed me that everything was shipshape. I then pointed to the airspeed indicator; since he was also a Thunderbolt pilot, he immediately realized that we were in this big airplane exceeding in level flight the allowed diving speed of the Thunderbolt at that altitude. This does not mean that the Rainbow had a higher critical Mach number than the Thunderbolt, but with the power we carried to that altitude we could reach a speed in level flight that would be too close to trouble for the Thunderbolt—which would have to be in a dive to achieve the same speed.

It may be confusing that the Rainbow is referred to as both the XF-12 and the XR-12. The former designation was used for early photographic aircraft. For the more sophisticated weapons systems the designation was changed to XR to indicate the broader concept. Some changes were made to convert the XR-12 to a transport plane, and we were able to guarantee a cruising speed of 450 mph for this version. Also the fact that the Rainbow would operate at 25,000 feet with any one engine out prompted one of the airlines to act to get the aircraft certified as a three-engine transport, so that a flight would not have to be aborted if one engine was feathered early in the flight.

Some of my remarks about the Rainbow may sound as if I were sold on it and just a little prejudiced. If so, I plead guilty as charged.

L. L. BRABHAM resigned from the Army Air Corps in 1940 to become a test pilot for Republic Aviation Corporation. He retired as vice-president of that organization in 1964 but still flies his Mooney Super 21 about 300 hours a year.